MW01107670

"*Words To Thrive By* offers an autobiographical road map for the seeking soul. Dorward's most painful experiences are tempered by time and love, leaving life-sustaining lessons in their wake."

— **Amanda Guinzburg,** *Huffington Post*

"It is rare that someone can take the events of their life, learn the lessons and then articulate those lessons so that another can benefit from their journey. Mary Anne Dorward has opened the door to her personal life lessons for you to benefit and hopefully illuminate your experience in the process called 'Life.' Her goal is for you to obtain meaning and relevance from everything that happens to you."

— **Cherie Carter-Scott, Ph.D., #1 bestselling author of** *If Life Is a Game, These Are the Rules: Ten Rules for Being Human*

"Mary Anne Dorward's chosen words have deep meaning for anyone striving to live an authentic existence. Her real life stories are magnetizing, riveting, dramatic, and still true, making her truth better than most fiction. *Words to Thrive By* is one of those books I want to have on hand to give my friends and my family because I know they will benefit from reading it.

— **Marjorie R. Barlow, Ph.D., author of** *The Possible Woman* **and** *The Possible Woman Steps Up*

"It is one thing to be inspired by another's words, but wholly another to be changed by them. As you read Mary Anne's extra-ordinary stories, life-changing adventures and pivotal moments that changed the trajectory of her life again and again, you can feel your own heart melting open to embrace the very pulse of Life. Allow this book to minister to your very soul. Allow it to change you. Be renewed and exhilarated by the vibration of love, reverence, awe, and deep gratitude that rolls off of its pages."

— **Debrena Jackson Gandy, bestselling author of** *Sacred Pampering Principles: An African-American Woman's Guide to Self-care and Inner Renewal*

"Mary Anne bravely and poetically explores how you can live your way into wholeness no matter what—and I mean, no matter what. This Handbook of Hope is personal and universal, inspiring and pragmatic. I enjoyed it immensely."

— **Jennifer Louden, bestselling author of** *The Comfort Queen's Guide to Life: Create All That You Need with Just What You've Got*

"Mary Anne's brilliance and zest for life comes through in the words in this dynamic book: ' 'Words are alive and powerful. The right word at the right moment can change anything…' It is a book of authenticity filled with soulful stories and reflections. I recommend it highly!"

— Gretchen Schodde, MN, ARNP, FNP-BC, Founder of Harmony Hill Cancer Retreat Center on Hood Canal

"Mary Anne Dorward has coached dozens and dozens of our members to help them gain public speaking confidence and find their real voices. In her new book *Words to Thrive By,* Mary Anne takes the next steps on this journey, capturing the profound experiences of her life—both the joyous and the deeply sorrowful—to illuminate the essential truths that we can all use to give deeper meaning to our lives. This is a book of power and possibility."

— Carla Lewis, President, Washington Women's Foundation

"I have been blessed with many teachings from my patients over the years. These are important life lessons learned during a time of a health crisis that they choose to share with me. These lessons include the wonders of life, the scare of death, the strength and peace of the soul. With greatest respect, gratitude and sincerity, thank you Mary Anne for the inspirations you have provided me and others through your book *Words to Thrive By.* I won't hesitate to recommend your book to my patients, my colleagues and my friends."

— Sandra Vermeulen, MD, Executive Director, Swedish Radiosurgery Center Swedish Medical Center, Seattle, Washington

"Be prepared for a ride from despair to joy. Be prepared to meet Mary Anne whose words of strength and courage will touch your heart and befriend your soul. Facing a hard time? Mary Anne has been there, too. Her book will be a reference work on your shelf for life."

—Alice Cunningham, Co-owner of Olympic Hot Tub Company

"As a man who would never buy a self help book, this is a *must* read."

— Tom Hujar, Founder and CEO of FDR Services, Political Consulting

For Cherie,
May the blessing of
abundant health and joy
be yours now and always!

WORDS TO THRIVE BY
POWERFUL STORIES OF COURAGE AND HOPE

Warmly,
Mary Anne Dorward

MARY ANNE DORWARD

Powerful Voices Press
• **Seattle, WA** •

POWERFUL VOICES PRESS

WORDS TO THRIVE BY

Powerful Voices Press
PO Box 51202, Seattle, WA 98115
www.powerfulvoicespress.com

To book Mary Anne Dorward for a speaking
engagement, visit www.myrealvoice.com.

FIRST EDITION

Book Cover Design by Anita Jones www.anotherjones.com
Interior Book Design by Aaron Busch www.aaronbusch.com

ISBN-13: 978-1466450417
ISBN-10: 146645041X

LCCN: 2011919042

To my children, Sarah and Joshua, and their children to come.
And to the memory of my son McKenzie.

Thank you for all I have learned from being your mother.

I love you, my cherubs…all three.

xoxoxo

Acknowledgments

To my dear Friends:

To quote Charles Dickens, it has been "the best of times and the worst of times." Thank you for always being there with me, no matter what.

Camille Ameen and **Ira Ingber**, **Abra Bigham**, **Richard Bingham**, **Gretchen Covey**, **Meg Cowles**, **Tom Hujar**, **Laurie McFadden Jones**, **Cyndi McDowell**, **Louise McDowell**, **Derek Mueller**, **Lisa Nakamura**, **Rev. Eric O'Del** and **Ken Fremont-Smith**, **Kieran O'Mahony**, **Susan Peck**, **Janaki Severy**, **Billie** and **Tim Taylor**, **Kathryn** and **Steve Vigar**, **Kippen** and **Eric Westphal**, **Colleen Willoughby** and in loving memory of **Catharina Gijlstra**.

To the Doctors, Hospitals and Therapists who saved my life:

Without each of you, I wouldn't have lived to tell this tale.

Northwest Hospital: Dr. Katherine Dee, Dr. Paula Denevan, Dr. Craig Hanson, Dr. James Joki, Dr. Sam Tolman and the Northwest Hospital Emergency Room Staff.
Swedish Hospital: Dr. Sandra Vermeulen
Virginia Mason Hospital: Dr. Ravi Krishnan, Dr. Craig Murakami and Dr. Ulrike Ochs.

Dr. Paul Amato, DDS, Dr. Anoosh Affifi, DDS, Genevieve Barile, LMP, David Calof, Dr. Ali Etemad, DDS, Robin Shapiro, MSW, Dr. C. S., Dr. Bryan and Cheryl Stewart, Dr. Guan-Cheng Sun and Dr. Kerong Xie.

To my immediate and extended Family:

You have each loved and supported me to the very best of your ability and have been instrumental in my growth. I am eternally grateful.

To The My Real Voice and Words to Thrive By Teams:

Each of you have brought your exceptional expertise to the ongoing creative collaboration of both the My Real Voice and Words to Thrive By Teams. Thank you.

Dave Buckley, Aaron Busch, Corinne Cavanaugh, Shelley Clark, Sam Gray, Elizabeth Harris, Anita Jones, Chris Malone, Derek Mueller, Stacey Stahl, Eric Weir, Wendi Wills, and Rachel Wirtz.

To My Children:

You make everything worth it.

Sarah Victoria Schenkkan and Joshua McHenry Schenkkan.

Table of Contents

Introduction

Words to Thrive By

Words are alive and powerful. The right word at the right moment can change anything. My favorite word is *courage*. I love the word *courage* because it tells us that even if we feel fear, get lost, or don't know what to do, we still have the capacity to triumph over any odds.

The word *courage* also brings to my mind the heroes and heroines of history who followed the great quests of old, who summoned something from deep within to overcome their obstacles. Then, the battle won, these heroes and heroines returned home with the knowledge, gift, or power that changed everything. I had a moment of profound awe and hope when I realized that the ability to overcome adversity is in each and every one of us: a wellspring of power, possibility, and determination that we can tap to wrestle the giants of our minds or slay the dragons of our experience.

The original definition of *courage* was: "to tell the story of who you are with your whole heart." This book is my story. This book is also your story, the universal, human story.

Despite the enduring myth of the strong, impenetrable Marlboro Man, we are, each of us, quite fragile creatures. Often we don't realize how fragile we are until something in our life suddenly goes sideways. That's when we turn to words to help us name our pain, celebrate our euphoria, or reframe our devastating experience to make it tolerable.

We turn to ministers, friends, or family for words of encouragement. We turn to our children or our sports heroes for words to describe amazement. We might even turn to Buddhism for its insights on how to begin the quest to find words for that-which-is-nameless. Some moments or profound experiences go beyond words altogether. At those times, we quietly hold each other or perhaps even howl in agony.

But the human spirit is an amazing thing. I believe that it is the Eighth Great Wonder of the World. If a human being has one whiff of hope, often given or received in the form of a word, sentence, idea, or story, that human being can carry on through the most difficult of circumstances, the most devastating grief, and the most profound of challenges.

My life has been anything but dull, peppered with stories of devastation and grief, faith and healing. But it doesn't matter who you are or where you live in the world; everyone needs tools to help them thrive. Writing this book has been my journey to wholeness. It is meant to be a Handbook of Hope, a map to inspire you to get to the other side of whatever road you are crossing, filled with the tools of life and laughter that we all need.

*****

Soon after I wrote this introduction, I participated in the traditional Japanese New Year's rice ceremony called *Mochitsuki*, at beautiful IslandWood, an unusual 255-acre outdoor learning center on Bainbridge Island, Washington. Island-Wood was originally designed to provide exceptional learning experiences. I certainly had an exceptional learning experience that day. I discovered that the *Mochitsuki* ceremony is the perfect metaphor for my life.

In the *Mochitsuki* ceremony, glutinous rice is soaked overnight and then cooked. The hot, cooked rice is then pounded hard over and over and over with large wooden mallets called *kine* in a traditional mortar called an *usu*. Eventually, the individual grains of rice have been pounded so much that they let go of their separateness and change into a smooth, sticky, opaque paste of rice dough. This soft, opaque white dough is twisted off and smoothed into balls called *mochi*. This *mochi* is then eaten with salty *shoyu* sauce, dropped into hot vegetable soup, or used to cover red bean paste, or ice cream and many other dishes.

Like the countless grains of rice in any batch of *mochi* in the *Mochitsuki* ceremony, all of us have had countless experiences. I have been pounded and pounded over and over again, and as a result, I am now much more smoother, more elastic, and more flexible. Just as I love each piece of *mochi,* different in shape or taste depending on what is around or inside it, the many experiences of my life have been tasty, some easier to get down than others, I'll admit. But each moment, each experience, has transformed me and helped me grow into who I am now.

I have learned that the painful pounding, stretching, and shaping I have endured is as important to my life journey as my moments of deep joy, laughter, and peace. Each experience, from devastating to glorious, has had its own measure of grace. Now, I just try to be open to what is present in each moment and allow all to be well, no matter what comes.

We are, each of us, a collection of stories. In the end, the words we choose to define any moment of our lives will be the legacy we leave behind.

Mary Anne Dorward
Seattle, Washington, 2011

Forgiveness

The Kiss

Forgiveness is complicated. I honestly did not know *how* complicated a concept this was for me—and others—until I began writing about it. Everyone, it seems, has a moving story about forgiveness in his or her life. And it doesn't seem to matter if the story is about giving it, receiving it, denying it, or being denied it. Forgiveness is powerful no matter which way the story goes.

Some people believe that there are things that others have done that are so horrible, they are unforgivable. Alexander Pope said, "To err is human. To forgive, Divine." I am saddened and somewhat embarrassed to admit that in writing this chapter, I have discovered that there are still people in my life who I am not yet able to fully forgive, despite what a Divine experience it would be for both of us. But, I'm working toward the goal of forgiveness, no matter how far off it might seem.

Choosing to remain angry about wrongs done to you by another makes every moment of your life a burden, and you remain hostage to both that person and what they did to you. The toxic effect of endlessly resenting another person and their negative actions is like swallowing a dram of poison yourself and wishing that other person would die. Not too terribly productive for either side.

But is forgiveness really essential to a peaceful and full life?

In a word, yeah.

*****

When I was eleven years old, I experienced my first kiss from a boy. Shawn was a very handsome boy from school. The setting was perfect. We were perched on a rock in the middle of a slow-moving river. I can still remember his lips touching mine. It was intense and wonderful. He kissed me again behind a tree at the top of the hill before we parted and we each went home. That second kiss was equally as wonderful as the first. What happened next still puzzles me: Why did I go to school the next day and tell everyone that Shawn was a rapist? As I look back, I have no idea what was driving this behavior. Was it a sense of guilt and/or shame that I had allowed a boy to touch me in some sexual way? But why not keep it a secret shame instead of tarnishing Shawn's reputation? I asked myself again and again, "Why did I do that to him?" I kept it in the back of my mind for thirty years. Finally, at our twenty-fifth high school reunion, I came prepared to find Shawn and make a long-overdue apology.

On the night of the reunion, I asked another classmate if Shawn was there, and he pointed him out in the crowd. He was still the best-looking man in the room. As I studied his calm demeanor, I was suddenly overcome with anxiety. My stomach did a nauseating flip-flop. I wondered if he would even remember me. It felt very risky to approach him, someone I had not talked to in thirty years, and simply launch into an apology.

I had to force my feet to walk the last few inches to where he was standing, dreading every step. This apology, I was sure, was going to be most humiliating. I wasn't sure exactly what I was going to say, only hoping to finally unburden myself by righting this wrong done to him many years before.

When I reached him, I stammered, "Hi, Shawn. You probably don't remember me." He looked straight at me. There was a cool energy in his eyes and only a flicker of a smile on his lips.

"Oh, yeah. I remember you, all right."

I thought to myself, *Oh dear, this is not going to go well.* I could feel my palms beginning to sweat and my face getting hot and flushed. I wanted to run, but my feet were lead and I couldn't. My lips moved.

"Shawn, I'm here to offer you an apology that I have owed you for the past thirty years."

His expression changed to a confused grin. "An apology? Whatever for?"

"I did something to you that I deeply regret. I have felt bad about it for a long time, and I am so sorry."

"Mary Anne, what did you do?"

His words shocked me. "You mean you don't remember?"

"Remember what? You have to know, MA, I did so many drugs during high school, I actually have no memory before the age of eighteen. That's one of the reasons I became a drug and alcohol counselor, to help other kids not turn out like me, with brain fry. So what happened? Now I am really curious!"

"Oh my gosh, Shawn, I can't believe this! I've been torturing myself about this thing I did to you for over thirty years and you don't even remember it! That would actually be pretty funny, if it didn't feel so tragic."

I took a deep breath and decided to finally just put it all out in the open.

"Okay, here's what happened. You kissed me by the river running behind the house at the end of our road and then again up behind the tree near the sidewalk. When I got to school the next day, I told everyone you were a rapist."

His face charged with uproarious laughter. He was laughing so hard, he nearly choked on his soda. "And you have been carrying around all this guilt for thirty years?" he managed to get out through the laughing.

"Well, yeah. I thought you hated me. I wondered what was wrong with me that I could do such an awful thing to you, when all you did was kiss me. Yeah. Thirty years of guilt." The release suddenly turned on me, and I couldn't stop the tears that had welled up.

"Wow," he said softly. "This has obviously really been hard for you."

"No kidding." I tried to calm myself by fumbling for a Kleenex in my purse.

"Well, I really have only one question." His face was serious again.

"What is it?" I asked, anticipating in complete dread. I was up to my ears in embarrassment already.

"Was it good?"

"Was what good?"

"The kiss. Was it good?"

I paused. Was I being forgiven or being made fun of? I looked in his face. Nothing but sincerity: he really wanted to know.

"Yeah. It was good," I said, sighing, and the memory of sitting on that big rock, with the sound of the rushing river, the smells of the eucalyptus trees, and the gentle, passionate kiss all came back in a flash. "Amazing, in fact. Yeah, I would have to admit in all honesty, it was actually *great*."

"Well, I'm really, really sad I don't remember it, then. Especially since that kiss was with as beautiful a woman as you."

"Thanks. But I really have to ask you, do you really forgive me? I assumed you have hated my guts all this time. "

"Actually, this conversation fills in a really important missing piece of my childhood for me. I'm sure glad to have that memory back."

"Wow. I feel so much lighter! Thanks!"

His hand touched mine. "Thank you...." And then he leaned down and kissed me again, right in the middle of the high school reunion. Thirty years later, it was every bit as good as the first time.

Ah, the sweetness of forgiveness.

*****

I imagine that most people would say that, given time and experience, there are things they would have done quite differently if they had them to do over again. We've all been there. But every hurtful thing done or said in our lives is an opportunity for the journey toward self-understanding and clarity of finding forgiveness—even if the only person who forgives us is ourselves. Most importantly, forgiveness of oneself and others provides a sense of closure: you can't change the past, but you can learn to let it go.

Fear and our inability to let go of difficult feelings of anger, frustration, humiliation, and shame make forgiveness seem difficult, if not—at times—impossible. We can all make the decision to not forgive certain people or not to let go of certain experiences, but that does not mean we ever lack the *ability* to do so. And in fact, the price of refusing to forgive can be very high. As I look back over my own life and the people or circumstances I have refused to forgive, it is not a pretty picture. It's taken me a long time to learn it, but I know now that it's up to me to change the way that picture looks.

I've bumped against walls of resentment as thick as the ones I'm trying to knock down in my own heart, when seeking forgiveness from others. When you go to someone and ask to be forgiven, you may not get what you wanted or hoped for. That person you harmed may not be able or willing to honor your request for forgiveness in that moment, if ever. Your request can open up a painful wound that the other person would just as soon leave alone or ignore. They are under no obligation whatsoever to accept your apology or honor your request for forgiveness. Being denied forgiveness, after all the courage it takes to ask for it, can be really painful. If that happens, then what do we do?

Forgiveness is a two-way street, and we take turns giving and receiving its gift throughout our life's relationships. Regardless of whether the other person is willing to walk down this street with us or not, at the very core of forgiveness lies the monumental opportunity that we each have to finally release ourselves and others from future torture and guilt. The very act of becoming introspective and stating out loud or on paper the harm you did, is a purifying moment of true perspective. To let another person know that you recognize that you have caused them pain, and letting that person know that you feel tremendous regret or sadness can become a great gift of personal redemption, relief, and release.

But, we are only responsible for opening this path, not coaxing the other person down it. When you take full responsibility for the fact that your actions have caused harm to another, you are freeing *yourself*, regardless of how the other person reacts. And if they should choose to carry their resentment past this point, you can hope that someday they get the relief you had the courage to offer. In our willingness to forgive rests one of the most powerful potentials we human beings have: the ability to gracefully receive closure and truly move on in our lives.

Over the years, I have tried to initiate conversations with each person I have wronged or who has wronged me in order to clear the air. This is the only way to take rotten potatoes, one by one, out of the sack on my back. Some conversations have turned out to be more productive than others, as the capacity to forgive and be forgiven is different for each of us. However the interaction turns out, it is always a relief to know that I have made the effort to clean up my side of the street. It is true that I cannot change another human being, but I can change myself.

Gratitude and humility are the beautiful bedfellows of forgiveness. I am grateful for those who have stepped up to forgive me for my failings or for wrongs I have done to them. And it has been a huge blessing to see the looks on the faces and sense the palpable relief in the people who have come to me for forgiveness. For those unresolved moments, and people needing my forgiveness or my needing theirs, I hope for the grace to see another opening for healing.

In the meantime, I shall remember that, like charity, forgiveness begins at home.

From Me
To You...

Try this. Look in the mirror and say "I forgive you" to your reflection. Even if you don't believe it now, someday you will.

Thank You, Brain

I keep wondering: what would it take for me to have just a little more patience with myself? How can I learn to give myself a little gesture of love, kindness, and gratitude now and then?

Sometimes, I order myself around as if I'm in some sort of a dog-and-pony show. It's chaotic and noisy as all the parts of my brain kick into gear, strutting their best stuff, all vying for equal attention and awards of notice and praise. I'm so exhausted just thinking about all I have to do.

It's no wonder I have a hard time listening to my own inner wisdom. Many days, I am moving too fast and there is too much noise going on in my head! As a result, my body, mind, and spirit suffer.

I'm trying to change that bad habit. Now, I try to think of one nice thing I can do each day to show my body that I appreciate all that it does for me. Every day I choose to send loving energy to a different part of my body: my heart, stomach, brain, blood vessels, hands, feet, face, and eyes.

All I do is say something like:

"I am grateful for all my heart does to keep me alive. Thank you, heart."

"I am grateful for my feet and where they carry me every day. Thank you, feet."

"I am grateful for my brain and all it does to help me think, create, and believe. Thank you, brain."

It's easy and so quick that I never have an excuse for leaving it out of my day.

When I am stuck at a red light and in a hurry, I patiently turn my attention to my breathing and say, internally or out loud, "I am grateful for all that I am," on an in-breath and "I am grateful for all that I have," on my out-breath. Or I might say on an in-breath, "God is my source." And on the out-breath I might say, "God is my supply." I'm always surprised at how this helps me begin to have patience for all the frustrations and delays that come up over the course of a day.

I actually look forward to delays now. A delay gives me a chance to practice my deep breathing and affirmations. And *any* time I am delayed, I am absolutely convinced that my Guardian Angel is protecting me from something—a car accident up ahead on the road, a person, or a bad energy I don't need.

And any time I find that I neglect this practice, I always regret it. Even if nothing specifically unpleasant happens, I might simply arrive where I am going with too little energy to fully enjoy the people and places I'm seeing. That is the biggest loss of all. However, if I am steeped in gratitude the entire day, my energy, and my peace feel boundless.

So I am grateful for all that I am and all that I have. Can you hear me breathing…?

From Me
To You...

Research shows that the average person has about 50,000 thoughts a day, and the majority of them are negative. Think about that for a second. We have 50,000 thoughts a day, and most are *negative*.

We can change this pattern of thinking.

It takes only twenty-one to thirty days of consistent practice to change a habit. If we slowly turn away from focusing on all the negative thoughts we have and begin to fill our minds with higher-energy concepts, words, and ideas, a new habit is born.

When we choose a new, more positive mental word-equivalent for the updated vision of ourselves that we want to create, we can begin to repeat it over and over, either silently or out loud. We can do this at any time over the course of our day, in the shower, in our car, in our meditation time, while walking, eating, or waiting in line at the grocery store.

As you think, so you shall be. When I feel I need more peace, I might say, "This moment is just as it should be." After breathing deeply and saying this even just a few times, I find that I do indeed feel more peaceful. When I want to feel more joyful, I say, "Every day in every way my life is getting better and better!" Repeating this phrase, it's not long before I feel more full of energy and have a sense of more joyful possibilities.

Affirming a sense of gratitude is also quite powerful.

"I am so grateful for all the love (or fulfilling work or friends or whatever feels right in the moment) in my life," is another great affirmation. Whatever you affirm and are grateful for draws more of that thing to you. What are you grateful for right now?

The Cross

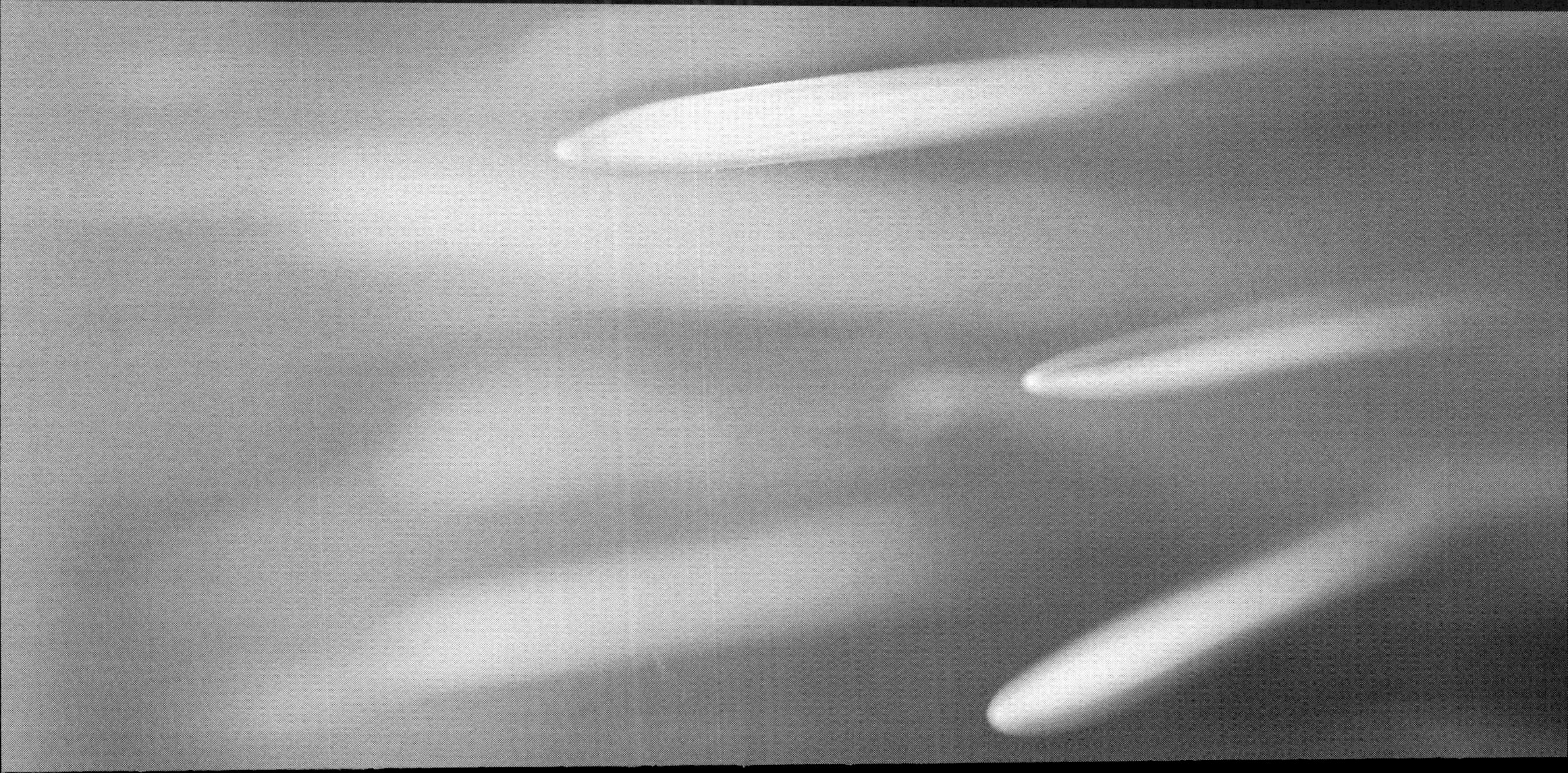

When I was four, my grandmother gave me a beautiful gold cross with hearts engraved on it. It was on a lovely gold chain, and I wore it night and day. I refused to take it off, even in the bathtub. I had a strong sense that this cross was protecting me somehow.

One day, a year later, I noticed that both my cross and chain were missing. I panicked. I asked my mother and brothers if they had seen them, but no one had. I felt disoriented and frightened without my cross around my neck.

I looked everywhere for my cross: in my room, my bed, the kitchen, and the TV room. As I retraced in my mind my steps to all the places I had been during the day, I suddenly realized I had been doing cartwheels on the lawn earlier in the morning. I raced for the front door, sure that both my cross and chain were probably in plain sight right there out on the lawn or the sidewalk.

When I walked out front, I gasped in horror. My father had just finished mowing the lawn. I ran to him and screamed, "Did you see my cross while you were mowing the lawn? Did you see my cross?" As he walked back into our house, he said that not only had he not seen it, but it was probably a lost cause by now. Then he stopped, turned around and said, "If that thing of yours is out there, I probably mowed over it. You'll never find it in all those grass clippings."

For a moment, I felt miserable and hopeless, like my heart had turned to stone and sunk into a deep, black pond. But then, suddenly, I had a new thought, and that new thought instantly changed my world:

Was I going to listen to him and give up, or was I going to force my mind to focus on a more positive outcome: finding my cross by giving my most determined shot to look for it?

I stopped, standing in the middle of the lawn, closed my eyes, and stood still for a few moments. I didn't realize at the time that this was my first moment of true meditation, of consciously contacting my deep Inner Knowing Self, the part of me that would guide me for the rest of my life. Standing in front of my house at age five, with my eyes closed, my intuition told me that I would find my cross if I tried.

With my eyes still closed, I mentally asked, "How?" The next thing I knew, I "saw" the image of a series of squares in my mind's eye. This "seeing" was as if I saw the page of a book in my mind showing what I now know to be a grid.

From this "picture" in my mind, I got the idea that if I created a system, like this series of boxes I saw in my mind's eye, somehow I would find my cross.

I looked at the vast expanse of my front lawn. It felt huge. But if I looked at it as a bunch of little squares, it seemed much smaller. "I'm the little engine that could," I told myself. "One square at a time, and I will find my cross. One square at a time. I can do this. I know it!"

I started in the far corner of the yard next to the hedge, as if I was in one corner of the grid I had seen in my mind. I got down on my hands and knees and began to pick through a square of grass just the width of my knees as if in a square and as far out as my arms would go. This was my "measurement" for one grid square. After I picked through the square within my reach, I moved my knees forward to look through another square block of grass.

Bit by bit, inch by inch, I got to the far side of the lawn. I had finished one long row of the grass grid, and there was no sign of my cross or chain. So I moved my knees over to my right, the width of another row of the grid, turned around and came back along the lawn inch by inch, square by square, until I reached the other end, which bordered the walkway.

After about an hour, my father came out and said, "Why don't you just give up? You'll never find it! What you're doing is ridiculous!"

I turned and looked up at him. I said evenly and with great determination: "No. If I keep looking, I will find it. I know I will find it."

"Well, I think you're wrong. You're wasting your time. You'll see." my father said, shaking his head. Then he added, "Hey, the boys and I are going swimming. Why don't you just go get your swimsuit and forget this whole thing?"

I gritted my jaw tightly, held my tongue, and shook my head in a silent "No." I believed I could find it no matter what anyone said. Looking back now, I can see that this was a huge moment for me in learning to believe in myself and trust my own gut.

So with an even firmer resolve, I went back to focusing on my task. Another hour passed. By now my brothers and my father had left to go swimming. My mother had stayed behind, and I could see from the corner of my eye that she periodically checked on me from the window. As time went by, and I had not found the cross, she came out and offered to buy me a new one.

"You know, Mary Anne, I'm sure we can find another cross just as pretty as that last one. We could go look right now!" I said, "Thanks, Mom, but I want the one Nonny gave me. And I'm not giving up until I find that one." She nodded, smiled, and went back into the house.

My brothers and dad returned soon after, and my father came out front and just laughed at me. "You're still out there looking for that stupid thing? Give it up, why don't you! It's hopeless!" I screamed for them to all leave me alone so I could stay focused and concentrate.

Another hour passed and I found a tiny link of chain. This was a very encouraging sign. If I found one link, the rest must not be far away! This discovery spurred me on to find the rest. Finally, I found my cross and the remains of my mangled chain. It was obvious that they had gone through the lawn mower and been spit out. The cross had a few scratches and dents and the chain was in ten pieces but I had found them.

With the cross and pieces of chain clutched in one hand, I lay on my back on the lawn and stared at the beautiful, blue sky. I smiled. I had proven to myself that my faith and determination would lead me to what I needed, no matter what anyone else said.

When I finally got up and screamed, "I found it! I found it! I found it!" it was my mother who came running out first. "Good for you! Good for you!" she yelled back, with a wide smile.

The day I found my lost cross taught me that if I believed in myself, I could accomplish anything. The vision of me on my knees looking for that very small cross has returned to my mind again and again over the years, especially when someone says, "That's impossible," or "You'll never find it," or "It will never work." Thanks to my Cross of Determination, "Just watch me," and "I can do this!" are what come to my mind first.

If you have a journal, this could be a great moment to reflect on your own life, letting your intuition show you where determination has shown up fully in your life. Or where it needs to.

So take a moment and sit down, close your eyes, take a deep breath, and relax. A feeling, a picture, some guidance or direction about your relationship to determination is waiting for you to discover it.

Respect

Chronic Interruptus

Abraham Lincoln once said, "There are those who listen and those who wait to talk." Do you notice how often in everyday communication it feels like the person in front of you is not really listening? Very often it seems like they are either waiting to talk or so impatient to give their opinions, they interrupt you mid-sentence. And isn't being interrupted while you are speaking really annoying and, at a deep level, disrespectful?

I do it all the time.

I know it's disrespectful to interrupt a person while they are speaking. But sometimes I just can't help myself. However, when we interrupt, we miss important and valuable parts of the other person that they were trying to share.

The fallout from being a "chronic interrupter" can really cost us, as well. In a personal setting, our family and friends may get so frustrated with our lack of listening skills that they may get angry or even just stop talking with us. In a professional setting, this habit of interrupting can cost us that promotion, that great yearly job review, and even our job.

So what is a "chronic interrupter" to do?

Step One: Observe Yourself

1. First, observe that interrupting people is a habit that you have.

2. Next, get a notebook to record your observations. You are beginning what I call the "Chronic Interrupter Field Research Project." In this notebook, you are going to keep a running list of who you interrupted, what they were talking about and what you felt inside when you interrupted.

3. Now pick a day, and for that entire twenty-four hours, jot down each time you interrupt people, whether they are friends, coworkers, or family members. Feel free to interrupt your family and coworkers as many times as possible. This is research, after all!

4. At the end of these twenty-four hours, tally up the number of times you interrupted someone. You may be shocked to find out at the end of a day just how many people you actually did interrupt in one day's time.

5. Now that you have your observation mode in full swing, take the next twenty-four hours and observe what is happening inside you

 and your head at the moment when you suddenly feel the urge to interrupt people in front of you. (Don't forget to write everything that comes up for you in your "Chronic Interrupter Field Research Project" notebook!) Stop, take a breath, and open up an observatory opportunity to mentally ask yourself questions while they are talking, such as:

- Am I bored with what they are saying and want to spice up the conversation a bit?
- Am I just SO much smarter than they are that I just need to set them straight on the facts or give another perspective on the subject?
- Am I feeling anxious that they know more than I do and want to get my own two cents in so they won't think I'm stupid?
- Do I think they're stupid and need to be straightened out a little?
- Do I just want to have the satisfaction of having the last word?
- Anything else?

Step Two: Observe Them

Now go ahead and interrupt them. While they are talking, observe very closely what happens to them when you interrupt and shut them down. Pay close attention to the following aspects of their body language at the moment you interrupt and as you take over the "conversation:"

- Notice the area around their eyes. Do they suddenly draw their eyebrows closer together into a frown? Do they suddenly blink fast a couple of times? Do they roll their eyes?
- Notice their hands. Do their hands close down into a fist, or do their hands suddenly look a bit more stiff, as if they were heading into a fist?
- Notice their mouth. Does it get a little more pinched-looking as you start talking over them?
- Notice their head. Do you observe a slight shake or tilt of their head to the side as you derail their thinking and insist that they switch to focusing on you and your idea?
- Do they have the courage to interrupt you back and tell you to stop talking until they are finished?

The person interrupted may be too polite to speak up, but all of these physical body movements outlined above, however slight, are body language indicators to you that the person interrupted is registering frustration or even anger at you for the interruption.

This "Chronic Interrupter Field Research Project" is designed to improve your communication skills and help you feel what it is like from another person's perspective. When they are interrupted, most people get very annoyed and give very clear physical signs of how frustrated they are at not being allowed to finish their thought.

Step Three: Let Them Finish

After you have completed the observations outlined above and have successfully observed the "interrupted conversation," both from your perspective and from theirs, pick the next person you are talking with and let him or her finish talking, no matter how frustrating and difficult it is for you.

- Do what you must in order to keep your mouth shut while the other person is talking. Pinch yourself, sit on your hands, kick yourself, imagine your lips are zipped or glued shut so you absolutely, positively will not interrupt them!
- Let the person finish, no matter what thought or urge to interrupt them comes up from inside you.
- Again, observe and be mindful of how it feels inside you to not interrupt. The first time you try to stop yourself from this habit of chronic interrupting could be quite difficult and challenging for you. Don't get discouraged. On average, research suggests that it takes twenty-one to thirty days to change a habit. You may need a few times and as many as thirty days to practice before you get it down.
- Is there any new information you observe coming up? If so, write it down.

Little by little, as you listen more and interrupt less, you will observe that there is more breathing space in your conversations with people. There is more give and take and more excitement in the exchange from both sides.

You may also begin to notice that as you interrupt less and people feel at ease knowing you will let them get their thoughts out fully, they will talk with you more about other aspects of their personal and professional lives. This kind of respectful exchange on a deep personal and professional level builds trust in a relationship. In some cases, friends, family, and coworkers will even begin to seek you out, and you may hear that they deeply value you for the quality of your listening.

There is another old wisdom saying that I really like: "God gave us two ears, two eyes and one mouth. And they should be used in that proportion!"

Consider using more of your eyes and your ears and less of your mouth. Who knows? You might really learn something!

From Me
To You...

Does someone interrupt you frequently? They might not even realize they are doing it. Let them know how it makes you feel.

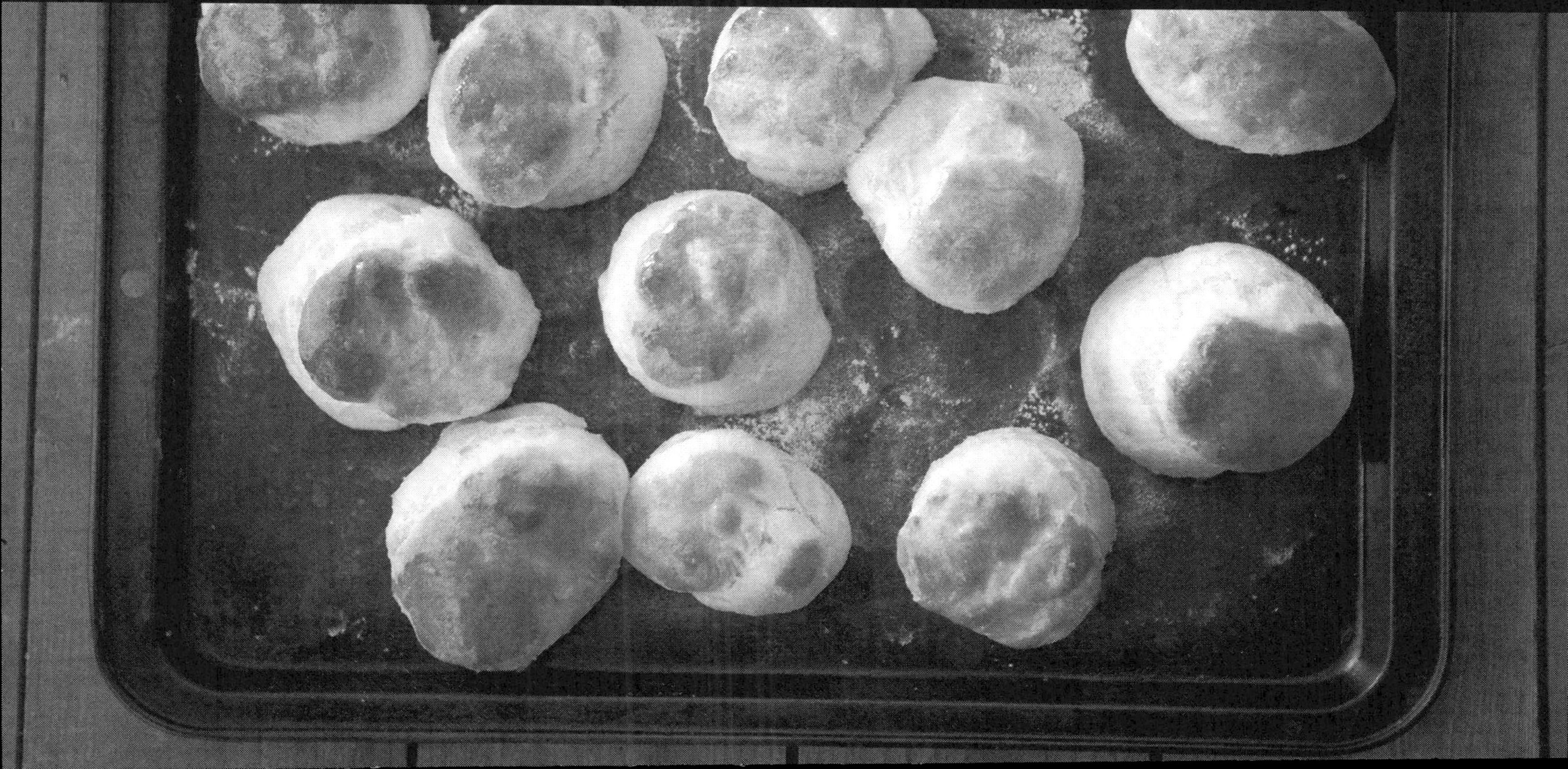

Comfort can come to us in all kinds of ways. Just like forgiveness, we take turns giving and receiving comfort all throughout our lives. Comfort can be given and received in the form of words, actions, and sometimes both.

When we give comfort, we reach into the world of another person and offer a perspective or an action that always has the potential to shift the person's focus to one of possibility. This comfort we offer to another can unlock that person's pain, suffering, or confusion. It can also help them to see their challenges as an opportunity for growth, learning, and even laughter.

When we need comfort, we must look within and ask ourselves what we really need at that very moment. Sometimes, finding comfort can be as simple as the distraction of a really good book or movie, a few hours of solitude, or a short nap. Some people find a lot of comfort at the gym. Just getting our bodies moving and willing ourselves out of our inertia into a class or a workout can bring comfort to both our minds and bodies. At other times, we need to motivate ourselves to reach out and ask for comfort through the companionship of others.

Some of my very best comfort conversations have taken place while a friend and I walked around nearby Green Lake. It is three miles around and takes about forty-five minutes for one full lap. I'll admit that some of my "comfort conversations" have required a couple of laps or more!

Finding comfort in life can be really challenging on some days. When the world looks grim and feels lonely, or we are totally lacking in motivation or feeling depressed, what are our options? Going to church or to a lecture to hear a new perspective, listening to music, or just getting ourselves out into nature can be some comforting choices.

I have to admit that when I need cozy comfort, Fluffy Tapioca Crème really does it for me. As long as I don't eat the entire batch all by myself, Fluffy Tapioca Crème always brings comfort to my body and soul. Some people refer to tapioca pudding as "fish eyes in glue." I assure you that if you follow the "Fluffy Tapioca Crème" recipe right off the back of the Kraft Minute Tapioca box, your tapioca pudding will be light and airy, and you will have fluffy clouds of meringue yumminess floating all throughout your bowl. It's always a comfort, no matter what is going on in my life. For me, "Fluffy Tapioca Crème" is, quite simply, Heaven on a spoon.

Other foods bring back great comfort memories of happy days. Artichokes always remind me of our family trips to Carmel-by-the-Sea every summer. Our family would stop along the way in Castroville, the "Artichoke Capitol of the World." We would walk out of the farmers stand with bags and bags of huge artichokes that always seemed as big as my head. I couldn't wait for my mother or father to get them going on the stove when we arrived home, and then an hour later, dunking them in melted butter or mayonnaise. Eating an artichoke has always been a very special delight for me. After pulling off, savoring, and arranging every leaf in a pattern on my plate, my artichoke ritual always ends with that scrumptious artichoke heart, which I always delay finishing as long as humanely possible. Every time I eat an artichoke, the taste takes me right back to my happy memories of being with my family in Carmel-by-the-Sea.

Some foods bring the comfort of the memory of people we love. My brother Steven had a coffee shop in California, and people used to drive for miles to buy his homemade scones. Whenever I make these for my family, they don't last long. In fact, if you plan to make these scones, you might as well make a double batch, since everyone who eats one will be begging for more! Feel free to share your favorite variations on my blog, WordsToThriveBy.com.

Here's the recipe:

Scones

Preheat oven to 395° F
Ingredients for one batch:

¾ cup heavy cream
½ cup unsalted butter (1 stick), frozen overnight
2 cups all-purpose flour
1 tsp baking soda
1 tsp cream of tartar
½ tsp salt
¾ cup sugar
1 cup fresh or frozen berries or sliced pears
Approximately 3 tsp turbinado sugar (such as Sugar in the Raw) for sprinkling on top, just before baking

(Note: turbinado sugar is a much coarser grind of sugar than is table sugar)

Instructions:

Preheat oven to 395° Fahrenheit.

In a bowl, combine flour, baking soda, cream of tartar, salt, and sugar. Sift combined ingredients. Sifting can be done with an old-fashioned sifter, or you can fluff it with a fork.

Grate a stick of frozen butter into dry ingredients and then toss with your fingers. This is a little like tossing a salad with your hands.

Next, form a well in the center of the mixed ingredients and pour in the heavy cream. Then toss again with the tips of your fingers to combine. The mixture should still be somewhat dry and not hold together.

Add one cup of fresh or frozen blueberries and toss throughout. My kids and I like the blueberry scones best, but try experimenting with raspberries, blackberries, marionberries, or any combination of fruits you have on hand, and see what you like best! Instead of folding the fruit in throughout the dough, you could also try placing some thinly sliced pears or nectarines around on top of your scone dough in a pinwheel pattern or any other arrangement  that inspires you. If you like, you can also leave the fruit out altogether. These scones are great plain.

Line a sheet pan with parchment paper, and pour the batter onto the parchment. It will be both crumbly and sticky.

Next, form the crumbly mixture into a flattened large round shape about eighteen inches in diameter. It will look like the size of a large pizza on the cookie sheet. Your large crumbly scone mixture circle should be about an inch high all the way around.

Next sprinkle the flattened round of scone batter evenly with the turbinado sugar. This coarser ground of sugar gives a lovely texture to the finished scones.

Bake at 395° F for 21–25 minutes or until golden brown. Do not over-bake! They look a little underdone when they are perfect. Cool to set. Once they are cooled a bit, cut the large scone circle like you would a pizza until you have six to twelve triangle shape slices.

These scones go beautifully with a rich, full-bodied coffee. My favorite coffee is Stumptown "Hair Bender" coffee blended into a vanilla latte with whole milk. Yum. Go to www.stumptowncoffee.com to order some or learn more about this wonderful Fair Trade coffee company. If I am in a tea mood, I love Stash Fusion Green and White Tea. You can order this tea at www.stashtea.com or you can find a box in the tea section of your favorite grocery store. I usually slice up some fruit—whatever is in season—on the side, and it makes a scrumptious and beautiful breakfast.

It doesn't matter whether you find comfort in a place, a person, a book, music, a food, or simply and quietly within yourself. Comfort is essential to a thriving life, whether you are the one giving comfort or receiving it.

From Me To You...

Among all his creatures in heaven or earth, God hath not made any like unto the sun in the firmament, the beams whereof are beautiful and pleasant, and do give comfort in all places to all things.

—John Jewel, English clergyman, 1522-1571

Courage

Mirror, Mirror

One of my most favorite movies is a subtitled German film called *The Lives of Others*. It's about the artists who were persecuted and their lives bugged before the fall of the Berlin Wall. The movie talks all about courage: the courage of artists defying the regime, and the courage and transformation of one man who was given the job of spying on them. In the beginning of the movie, the German officer characters talk about the protocol for breaking the will and spirit of an artist during the war. The interrogators had found over time that the most effective method was to keep the artist or writer awake and in isolation for extended periods of time. Very soon, they discovered, they could get the answer to any question they wanted, as well as the added bonus of having broken the artist's will to create any subversive or politically charged material.

This makes a lot of sense to me. Though never physically tortured, I have been through several periods in my life when I was mentally tortured, deprived of sleep and the basic human contact everyone needs to be happy. I don't care how powerful a person thinks they are; even the strongest among us can be broken down. And the converse is also true. Some extremely strong-willed people can go through tremendous torture and not ever give in or give up. Rather, they seem to get stronger and more filled with the wisdom of valuable experience that they later draw upon to help themselves and others. What is the difference between one person whose power can be broken and another whose cannot? It seems this is an inside journey that each person must take for themselves.

I once had a dream vision in which I held a hand mirror up to my face and gazed at my reflection. In my dream vision, I watched myself smash my reflection in the mirror, sending all these tiny, sparkly glass pieces of my face flying up into the air and then floating down, until the entire mirror was in a million, jagged pieces all over the floor. As I stared at all the tiny pieces, it became clear that each one contained a fragment of an important part of me from specific moments of my life, from my birth to now.

Then in my dream vision, I watched myself get down onto my hands and knees and gather up all the pieces of my life into a big pile in front of me. As I picked up each piece of my life mirror, one at a time, I noticed that, curiously, the glass did not cut my hand at all. I looked tenderly at myself in each jagged piece of the mirror, reviewing each memory contained within each different piece. I could see both the reflection of my face now and also a picture of my life experience represented by that piece from that year.

Then, one by one, I painstakingly placed each jagged piece of mirror back into the mirror frame. Though a fractured mosaic, each individual piece of memory seemed to fit somehow, as if my entire life was now a kind of jigsaw puzzle. Eventually, all the pieces were in place, and the mirror frame was easily and perfectly able to hold them. Then I slowly brought the mirror to eye level to see my own reflection.

When I held the mirror with the jagged pieces up to my face, I felt somehow even more beautiful in all those jagged little pieces than when there was only one individual large reflection of me. It was so curious.

When I described it all to David, my therapist at that time, he smiled a wide smile. "Wow. Do you remember when you first came in here and how frightened you were to face yourself?"

"Yeah, I sure do. I hated myself, and I was sure I would hate myself in the end, too. But it was so bizarre in this dream vision. When I finally had the nerve to really look at myself in the mirror, even with all these jagged and fractured little pieces, I had this feeling of respect, somehow. There was also a feeling of admiration, even, for going through all I have been through and not ever giving up. I just loved myself. And strangely enough, it didn't feel egotistical at all. When I held that jagged mirror up to my face in my dream vision, I didn't feel ugly or a failure or stupid at all, even with all those tiny little smashed pieces. Everything seemed to have a place. There was just this deep acknowledgment of all the incredible hardship I had overcome and the courage I had needed to face it all, slowly, bit by bit. But that's just my interpretation. What do you think it means, David?" I asked.

"I think it means you are finished with therapy. Have you ever thought of writing a book?" David grinned.

From Me To You...

Journals: Along the way I have found journals very useful in the journey to the center of my soul. My favorite brand of journals is the Moleskin journals with the hard black covers. I like these because of their solid cardboard backs that support writing on both sides of the page: www.moleskineus.com.

Meditation: As I wrote in the story, I have found meditation very helpful along my journey. If you have never meditated before, you don't really need to take a class. Just close your eyes and breathe. Try to let the thoughts come and go, and pay attention to the spaces between the thoughts. Gradually the spaces will become longer and the thoughts shorter.

While on this journey, whether you have never meditated or you have meditated for years, it's important to remember: "If your mind is empty, it is always ready for anything: It is open to everything. In the beginner's mind there are many possibilities; in the expert's mind there are few."
–Shunryu Suzuki, *Zen Mind, Beginner's Mind*

Books: One meditation book I have really benefitted from is Raymond Holliwell's book, *Working with the Law*.

Another helpful book on meditation is *An Easy Guide to Meditation for Personal Benefits and Spiritual Growth: Techniques and Routines for All Levels of Practice and Holistic Lifestyle Guidelines*, by Roy Eugene Davis.

Your Stories of Courage: If you have a story about courage and would like to share it with me and others, I encourage you to send it to me at **www.WordsToThriveBy.com.** I'm a firm believer that we are all in this together and that by sharing our stories, we can help each other along our way.

Sideways Blessings

I CAN wade grief,
Whole pools of it,—
I'm used to that.
But the least push of joy
Breaks up my feet,
And I tip—drunken.
Let no pebble smile,
'T was the new liquor,—
That was all!

—Emily Dickinson, Poem 35

One day in English class, long ago I was covering both my face and my paper with my left forearm as I laid my head down on my desk trying to write. But no matter how hard I tried, I could not stop my tears from falling on my assignment, blurring out the blue ink on the college-ruled paper. Out of the corner of my left eye, I could see my teacher standing beside me. I did not want anyone, least of all Mr. K, to see that I was crying. So I bent a little farther forward, hoping he would move on to another student. He didn't.

Finally, I looked up at him. He was standing there, smiling his gentle smile that turned up at the corner. There was a pause. Then he said simply:

"Ms. Dorward, there is a quotation that you might find appropriate at this moment."

"Well I hope so, Mr. K, sir. Nothing else seems to be helping much."

"I see that. Please listen carefully: 'I can wade whole pools of tears, but a drop of joy sends me tippling.'"

There was a moment and then I said, "Well, Mr. K, I'm not tippling much right now am I?" gesturing to my assignment on my desk, which was now one big, wet blob of spreading blue ink.

"Perhaps not, Ms. Dorward. Perhaps not today," Mr. K said kindly. "Perhaps not even next week or even next year. You may not believe it now, at this moment, but we can wade through all those pools of tears. You will."

"I hope so. God, I hope so." I said in a whisper, shaking my head.

"Ms. Dorward?"

"Yes, sir?"

"I can assure you that the day will also come when you will feel much more than a drop of joy and you will know the meaning of tippling. I promise."

*****

The Joy Ambassador for Cancer

Later in my life, as a five-time cancer survivor, I became known as the Joy Ambassador for Cancer.

Mary Anne Dorward
Speech Delivered at Amazing Grace Spiritual Center
Seattle, Washington, USA
October 4, 2009

Good evening. I'm Mary Anne Dorward and the title of my talk this evening is: GOD'S GRACE THROUGH CANCER.

I am a cancer survivor.

Two years ago in 2007, I was operated on for pre-cancer on my face and then had surgery for cancer in my leg.

The highlights of 2008 were that I was raped, I was in a near-fatal cycling accident, and my dog, bird, and favorite female relative all died.

And now in 2009, two months ago, I was operated on for cancer on my cervix and in my breast, and I have just started the first of what will eventually be thirty-three radiation treatments. Now you might be thinking, "What a rough few years!" And you would be correct. It was.

And during these past three years, there have also been what I call, "sideways blessings," and such incredible evidence of God's grace. That is what I would like to speak about with you tonight.

When I first heard the big C word, "CANCER," my first thought was DEATH. If it were written out as an irrefutable mathematical equation, it would be C = D. Cancer equals Death.

However, now I'm thinking that cancer is the best thing to ever happen to me. Why?

Well, honestly, I wasn't really listening to my body or my heart, both of which were screaming for my attention and love. Now I'm listening.

Cancer has also given me the permission I needed to communicate in ways I never would have before, both with myself and with others. In fact, cancer has completely transformed my life.

For me, C now equals C: Cancer = Communication.

Here are just three examples of how cancer has provided an incredible opportunity for communication and also has completely transformed my life:

1) I am finally listening to my body, and I no longer allow toxic people, food, ideas, or belief systems into my life.

2) Over the past three years, I have researched and learned everything I could about cancer and what causes it. As a result, in my treatment choices, I have done my best to combine not only the best of both the Western and Eastern medicine traditions, but also the best of the naturopathic medicine and raw-food movement, as well.

   What I know now is that if you have to have cancer, now is the best time in the history of the world to have it! Not only has the technology improved dramatically, there are also so many wonderful treatment options now that we all have to choose from!

   And I know from my own experience, with God's grace we are each more than capable of completely healing ourselves!

3) Best of all has been my Journey of Healing from within. I have a new relationship of Love, Compassion, Kindness, and Joy within myself that was never there before. I am now truly a JOY Ambassador everywhere I go.

So, how in the world does a person become a JOY Ambassador for cancer?

Well, every day I say to myself, over and over and over again: "There is only one life. That life is God's life. That life is perfect. That life is my life now. I am a Joy Ambassador and choose to learn all my lessons through Joy. From Joy, I was born. In Joy, I abide, and to Joy, I shall return."

And the results have been fascinating and fun. Everywhere I go along my Healing Journey, people are commenting that they have never seen anyone embrace

their cancer journey with so much courage, good humor, and joy.

In Conclusion

So what are some of those "sideways blessings" I referred to earlier?

Well, without the bike accident fifteen months ago, which caused me 24/7 excruciating pain, the doctors would never have given me an MRI this past July. The MRI is how the two breast cancer tumors were discovered. As a result, the doctors caught my breast cancer early, before it even showed up on a sonogram or mammogram. As a result, I have been given a 90–95 percent full-recovery prognosis.

My mother, on the other hand, was not so lucky. She was diagnosed and had a mastectomy at age fifty-five, four years older than the age I am now. She was dead, riddled with breast and bone cancer, just five years later at age sixty. So I am grateful to be alive here to tell you this story!

Things are not always what they seem.

At first that painful, scary bike accident fifteen months ago looked like the worst thing that had ever happened to me. Now it looks like a "sideways blessing," the "miracle," that actually saved my life. So, again, things are not always what they seem. "I" am not "my cancer." I am a spiritual being who has had several physical experiences of cancer.

I am so convinced that God is so totally in charge of my life, I have now completely released my fear of death.

I am listening to myself and my own wisdom for the first time in my life, instead of listening to a hundred other people ahead of my own gut instinct.

And now as a result, finally, after fifty-one years, I totally trust myself.

I have released my need to relentlessly push myself.

I live in peace and joy.

I am grateful.

And God is the Wholeness I am.

Thank you!

*****

Since that speech in 2009, I have overcome another nest of cancer tumors in my face and then plastic surgery to repair the three-inch hole the removal of that cancer left behind, I have overcome a severe bone infection in my jaw bone and surrounding tissues, I have had to have bilateral knee surgery to repair two badly torn meniscuses, and then I have dealt with a 6.5-inch post-surgery blood clot that could have killed me.

In July 2011, I slipped and fell down the stairs outside my apartment and knocked myself out on the concrete below. By the time I "came to," I had a severe concussion and sprained neck, shoulder, and ankle.

Each time a new challenge arose, I tried very hard to remind myself that, "This too shall pass." On the days when the pain was excruciating beyond belief, I would just tell myself to keep taking another breath and then another and then another. Some days that was all I could do. It had to be enough.

Although it was another hard year, and many people have told me that they could never have gotten through all that I did, I still have my sense of humor intact. Every day I shake my head in wonder that I am still alive to tell this tale. Throughout this difficult journey, I took great comfort in the words of the blind and deaf educator, Helen Keller: "We could never learn to be brave and patient, if there were only joy in the world."

So in the end, my English teacher, Mr. K, was right. Even through a life of dark and challenging circumstances, I have felt more than a tiny drop of joy, and my tippling continues.

From Me
To You...

I have always enjoyed the writing of the Irish dramatist and socialist, George Bernard Shaw. I totally agree with him when he talks about what the true joy in life is:

"This is the true joy in life, the being used for a purpose recognized by yourself as a mighty one; the being thoroughly worn out before you are thrown on the scrap heap; the being a Force of Nature instead of a feverish selfish little clod of ailments and grievances complaining that the world will not devote itself to making you happy."
—from his play, *Man and Superman, Epistle Dedicatory*

Ask yourself, what is your purpose, recognized by yourself, as a mighty one?

What is one small step you can take today that will lead you closer to your own mighty purpose and to becoming a true Force of Nature?

Inspiration

From the Outside, In

Finding inspiration can be the labor of a lifetime, or it can happen in an instant. Inspiration is an extraordinary feeling, whether it comes from a book that changes our perspective, from a person who lifts our spirits, or from simply being out in nature. The impact of a sudden inspiration can change your entire day. Whenever someone talks and hits the nail right on the head about a particular subject, a parts of my head and heart feel like they explode simultaneously. Positive inspiration brings me great joy.

But when the bottom falls out and I am personally lacking in inspiration, or I feel that my spirits are flagging, I turn to my bookshelf. Sometimes a particular book catches my eye, and I pay close attention to which section or shelf I feel drawn to. This is true in bookstores, as well. At times, books have seemed to jump off the table or shelf in Barnes and Noble or at the East West Bookstore, here in Seattle.

Sometimes I even create an inspiration field trip of several hours, where I go to the bookstore and wander around until I feel drawn to a particular book or section of the bookstore. There I wait to see which book "speaks" to me. I pick that book up and open it to discover what surprises of inspiration lay in store for me. I have always found these inspirational field trips fun and fascinating.

When a book *does* seem to jump out at me, I pick it up and flip it open to a random page. I imagine that I am in a conversation with God or my Guardian Angel, and this is Their way of getting a special message to me that I need at that moment. I absolutely love that special pull towards a new book. Reading for an hour or so is just a delight. Some days, it feels like a spiritual class designed especially for me!

When no book makes itself known, or I don't have the time to get to the actual bookstore, I choose some of my favorite books from my own bookshelf. I take them with me over to my meditation chair or my couch or bed and just open to my favorite sections. It always feels very comforting to me to be with my books, whether they are poetry or prose. In this new age of information and virtual communication, sometimes my inspiration comes over the Internet through my inbox on my computer.

Not long after I moved from my home to an apartment, I was having a rather down day. Even though I adored being close to the sea and it was a dream come true, that day I just felt a little sad as I sat alone in my new place. It was jammed floor to ceiling with unopened boxes, and I was feeling lonely and overwhelmed. Suddenly I felt inspired to go over to my computer and check my inbox. Boom, there was an e-mail from my dearest friend, Kath. When I read the title of the e-mail, I was rather stunned:

> "Daily Om: Where the Soul Is Finding the Place You Belong. Moving locations when you feel strongly to do so is a way of bringing your spiritual and earthly energies together."

Wow, I thought to myself. *Wasn't I just thinking to myself how overwhelmed I was feeling about moving?*

Well, of course, then I had to read the rest of Kath's "Daily Om" e-mail message:

> There will likely be times in your life when your soul evolves more quickly than your circumstances. Your subconscious mind may be ready to move forward long before you recognize that you are destined to embrace a new way of life. Your soul intuitively understands that changing habitats can be a vital part of the growth process and that there may be one part of you that is eager to move to another home.
>
> If you find it difficult to move on, consider that just as people in your life may come and go, your role in others' lives may also be temporary. And many of the conditions that at first seemed favorable served you for a short time. When you are ready to match your situation to your soul, you will find that you feel a new sense of harmony and increasingly connected to the ebb and flow of the universe.
>
> Moving on can be defined in numerous ways. Your forward momentum may take you from your current locale to a place you instinctively know will be more nurturing, comfortable, and spiritually enriching… and you will know that you have found a sanctuary.
>
> Clarity may come in the form of a question if you are willing to seriously ask yourself where your soul is trying to take you.
>
> In a way, moving from one point to another when you feel strongly driven to do so is a way of bringing your spiritual and earthly energies together. It is a two-step process that involves not only letting go but also reconnecting. You will know you have found your destination, physical or otherwise, when you feel in your heart that you have been reborn into a life that is just the right shape, size, and composition.

This message could not have been more perfect for me at that moment. Now that I have lived in my apartment for a little over a year, I have found it to be a cozy sanctuary and just the right size and shape for me.

It seems now that my soul knew before I did that I needed to move here, to this particular spot, in order to find peace, balance, and the inspiration to finish my book. This spot right on the water has helped me gain all kinds of other forms of inspiration, too.

Every day as I sit writing, eating, or resting, and I look out at the beautiful, ever-changing, Northwest nature, I feel such an overwhelming sense of gratitude for the beauty that now surrounds me. Every day I get to watch the ebb and flow of the Puget Sound tides, the pair of eagles with a nest in a nearby tree, and the boats of all shapes and sizes that come and go through the Ballard Locks at all hours of the day and night.

Every day I wake up to the delicious scent of the ocean, and it reminds me of the vacations our family took to Carmel every summer, which I just loved. I have actually never been happier living anywhere in my life. I love every minute in my little piece of heaven on earth.

Having said that, there are times when I still must find different ways to create inspiration for myself. I rent a movie or I might go search online for quotes. Here are two of my favorite quotes that have always inspired and comforted me:

"The difference between the right word and the almost right word is really a large matter. It is the difference between lightning and the lightning bug."
　　—Mark Twain

Beannacht ~ (Blessing)

> …On the day when
> the weight deadens
> on your shoulders
> and you stumble,
> may the clay dance
> to balance you.
>
> And when your eyes
> freeze behind

the gray window
and the ghost of loss
gets into you,
may a flock of colors
indigo, red, green
and azure blue
come to awaken in you
a meadow of delight.

When the canvas frays
in the curach of thought
and a stain of ocean
blackens beneath you,
may there come across the
waters
a path of yellow moonlight
to bring you safely home.

May the nourishment of the
earth be yours,
may the clarity of the light
be yours,
may the fluency of the
ocean be yours,
may the protection of the ancestors be yours.

And so may a slow
wind work these words
of love around you,
an invisible cloak
to mind your life.

—John O'Donohue, from his book,
Anam Cara, ("Soul Friend" in Gaelic)

A Field Trip

I hope that this book will be an inspiration to you to find your own peace and inspiration.

However, on a day when you feel blue or cannot see your life clearly, try this: create a field trip day. Remember how much we used to look forward to that as kids? But **this** field trip is where you go to a nearby bookstore and give yourself permission to roam around until a particular section draws your attention. See what bookshelf attracts you or gives you the feeling of "Hmm, this could be interesting." Then go to that section, choose a book at random or, again, one that captures your attention, and open it. If it feels interesting, find a chair or stepstool in the bookstore and start reading. See what inspiration and wisdom is just waiting there for you.

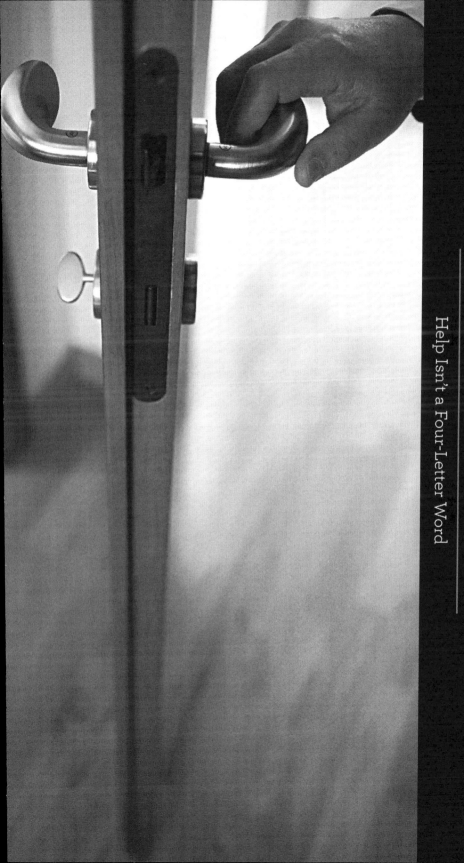

Help Isn't a Four Letter Word

For my fiftieth birthday, I flew to Brazil to meet a healer named John of God. The Casa de Dom Inácio (The House of Saint Ignatius Loyola) is a spiritual healing center in Abadiânia, central Brazil. Here, for over twenty years, João Teixeira de Faria, a gifted and powerful medium known as "João de Deus" (John of God) has helped countless people achieve miraculous healings—of cancer, AIDS, paraplegia, blindness and many other serious or seemingly "incurable" illnesses.

In my own research and conversations with people who had been to Brazil to meet John of God, they all spoke with great reverence about this truly humble man, quietly doing God's work of healing in our world. As result, I decided to go meet him and see for myself. I figured that if John of God could heal other people of incurable things, perhaps he could also heal my hardened heart and my seemingly incurable feelings of rage.

I cashed in all my frequent-flyer miles for a first-class ticket to Brazil, and three months later, in January 2008, I was sitting on a plane heading halfway across the globe. Three planes and eighteen hours later, I was flying over the Amazon River as it snaked down through Brazil en route to Sao Paulo. Later that day, I boarded another smaller plane which finally landed in the current capital of Brazil: Brasilia.

The next morning we met our tour guide, Heather Cummings. She was a tall, attractive woman in jeans and cowboy boots. Heather was all business. She would be our guide and translator throughout the trip.

There were eight of us in the minivan as we wound up into the high hills toward Abadiânia, the place where the Casa and our hotel, or *pousada*, were. When we arrived at the *pousada*, my room felt a little like a monk's cell: two twin cots, each with a very thin mattress pad, one blanket, and one sheet. There were no pictures on the wall and only a rod in one side of the room to hang up my clothes. This was to be my place to sleep and meditate for the next two weeks.

After we unpacked a bit, a few of us decided to walk over to see the Casa, where we would be going for our first meeting with John of God the following day. We left the *pousada* and began walking toward the Casa on the dirt road, which was a beautiful deep red-brown color. As we walked, horse-drawn carts passed us filled with colorful vegetables passed us. People smiled. We smiled back.

The Casa is a simple building with simple furnishings. On the days when John of God does his healing work, it fills with people from all over the world, speaking many languages. Hundreds of people arrive on crutches, in wheelchairs, by bus or car or bicycle. Some people in need of healing are carried in by others, and some walk under their own power. It reminded me of the time of Jesus, when the crowds were said to gather in order to be healed.

To many people, John of God is considered one of the most gifted healers living today. While he calls himself Juan de Taxeo, or John from the city of Taxeo, most people refer to him as John of God. He says that he himself does not heal, but that God works through him. People speak of his many miracles. Many people, even heads of state from around the world, return every year in gratitude for the healings their friends, family, colleagues, and they themselves have received. They come to sit and bring healing energy to help others, not asking for a healing themselves.

The next morning, one by one, we were each given an opportunity to meet and speak with John of God. We had been told to come prepared to ask a question that we would like some help with.

As I came within five feet of John of God sitting in his wooden rocking chair, I burst into tears. I thought to myself, *Well, if this guy can see deep into me and heals at the deepest possible level of any of my diseases, then I'm kinda worried. What if he can see absolutely everything about me? That could be really bad! What if I am incurable? What then? Would he tell me?*

Then my thoughts took a different turn: *I guess there is nowhere to run and nowhere to hide at this point! I might as well stay in line and see this thing through.* But I felt so inexplicably moved, and my tears were coming so fast that one of the Casa assistants to John of God handed me a big wad of Kleenex. I tried to smile. I thought about bolting from the room, but found I could not.

When I got to the front of the line, I took John of God's hand and dropped to one knee. Looking up into his face, I could not believe the intense color of his eyes. He had the deepest, glacier-blue eyes of anyone I had ever met. John of God looked deeply at my face for a few moments and then back to Heather, the translator. Heather asked my question, which I had written on a piece of paper: "With all my gifts and talents, where do I serve God best?"

John of God looked back at me, then back to Heather and then asked her a question in Portuguese that I did not understand.

While they were talking, I continued to kneel on one knee and to hold John of God's hand, as Heather had instructed me to do. I noticed that John of God kept turning his gaze back to me, then back to Heather in a deeply penetrating way.

I waited for what seemed like a long time. Minutes were ticking by; the conversation between Heather and John of God was getting more and more intense and louder and louder. I leapt to the worst possible conclusion.

Oh no. Maybe he can see that I am much sicker than I realized. What if this means something really bad? My eyes went back and forth between the translator and John of God, unable to understand a word and getting more nervous by the second. Finally, John of God waved his hand, said something emphatic to Heather, and waved me on.

Heather had no time to explain what had been going on, only to whisper, "Sit over here. He wants you to sit in his current."

"His current? What's that?" I whispered back.

"Just find a chair close by and go into meditation. I will explain later."

For the next two hours of seated meditation, the many variations of *What if this?, What if that?, What if...?* rang through my ears over and over. Finally, the Lord's Prayer, the Prayer of Caritas, and the Hail Mary signaled the end of the three-hour meditation session. I got up and went outside to have a bowl of soup and bread that I was told had been blessed by John of God and was also an important part of a person's healing process while at the Casa. I was exhausted.

When I finally found Heather outside, I asked, "It seemed like you and John of God were having some strong words or an argument about me, or something. So what did he say?"

Heather smiled. "Oh, don't worry. John of God asked me what you were doing with your talents right now. I told him that you taught politicians and executives how to speak with their hearts. And John of God wanted to know if you knew Hillary Clinton. I told him no, you didn't, but that you had met Bill Clinton."

I was dumbstruck. I thought to myself: *Politics? That's the absolute last thing I thought I would be discussing in Brazil with John of God. I want to get* out *of politics, not further into it!*

"So then what did he say?" I asked.

"Well," Heather continued, "John of God said he wanted you to sit in his current, and he also wants to do a special spiritual intervention on you this afternoon. So please don't be late to the afternoon session at the Casa."

That afternoon I went in for a "spiritual intervention." I really had no idea what that meant. I had read in Heather's book about others' experiences and had talked with other people at the *pousada*, but you really cannot imagine what it is like until you, yourself, have been through it.

At the Casa, we walked in the doorway to the first room and rounded the corner to the current room, then walked through to the surgery room. I sat down with about sixty other people who were also there to receive a "spiritual intervention." I closed my eyes and waited for something to happen, even though I wasn't sure what it would be.

As soon as my eyes closed, my face felt as if it had been numbed by anesthetic. Then I felt a pressure around both of my eyes, like a cut, only it didn't hurt—like when the dentist is working in your numbed mouth. Then it felt as if the skin under my eyes was being peeled back. Then the same thing happened over both breasts and also on my right side. It felt very strange.

When we were told that the spiritual intervention was completed, we stood up to leave. Later, I asked how long we had been there and was told it had been a total of an hour of sitting. I was surprised. At the time, it had felt like only ten minutes. As I left the building, I became aware that I could not see very well. My vision was blurry, the light really hurt my eyes, and this scared me. I went to Heather for help, and she handed me a pair of dark glasses to help me tolerate the afternoon light.

Heather got me into a cab, which took us over to the Casa pharmacy to pick up our herbs and then back to the *pousada* to rest. We were told to be as still as possible for twenty-four hours and then return to the Casa for a check-in.

Heather also told me that since I had received spiritual intervention on my eyes, the Casa protocol was that I should not read or do anything else with my eyes for a full eight days, which would allow my eyes the necessary time to heal. I was dumbstruck. Eight days doing absolutely *nothing*? This left me with the choices of sleeping, eating, meditating, and being quiet for a full eight days. I was fairly sure that I would die without any distractions.

Was she kidding? was my first thought. *I am a workaholic. I have to do some-thing. I can't just sit around and meditate and eat and sleep for a* week! *And I most certainly cannot be silent. I'm sorry. That's not possible.*

But those were the instructions. I went back to Heather and said, "This can't possibly be what John of God wants me to do."

She shook her head and said, "If John of God gives clear instructions, as he did to you, I would suggest strongly that you follow them. His instructions here at the Casa are the equivalent of a doctor's prescription in the United States. Only you are going through not only a physical but also an emotional and spiritual healing. Don't worry. We'll bring your food to your room."

The first few hours in my room were excruciating, with pain beginning to rise in all the areas that I had felt "surgery" happening. The first day was okay, as I was pretty tired, but after that it began to get more and more challenging. On day two, I ran into a fellow guest in the hall when I was going downstairs to get a cup of tea.

"Hurt?" he said.

"Yeah. Everywhere I had 'surgery' hurts," I replied, wincing.

"It really helps if you put some of the holy water from the Casa on those places. I always find the pain totally goes away when I do that."

"Gee, thanks," I said. "I'll try that."

After I got my tea and went back to my room, I tried putting the holy water John of God had blessed onto the "surgery" sites on my face, breast, and side. Within a matter of moments, all of my pain was gone. It was all very bizarre. But at least I finally drifted off to sleep.

The next day, I still had nothing to do but sit or lie there, and I had no one to talk to. I felt like I was imprisoned in a monk's cell with no break for mass. I couldn't go outside, read, or listen to music on my iPod. Three days into it, I hit the wall. I began to cry all day and night for reasons I did not understand. I could not sleep, either, and my life became a living nightmare, day and night. I wondered how this could possibly be considered a healing experience.

One day, after struggling for a good eight hours, I had had it. I was angry, tired, and frustrated. I was also very stuck. I went back to Heather's room and slipped a note under her door: "I am going absolutely out of my mind. Can you please come to my room, ASAP?"

Not long after, Heather arrived and sat down on the other twin cot in my room. I proceeded to unload a bucket of rage and resentment: "I don't *get* this. I don't know what John of God *wants* from me! I don't know *what* to *do* to *free* myself from all this *anger* I feel. I've been angry my entire life. I can't do this! I'm clearly a failure at this healing thing. I'm sure that John of God will think I am an *idiot! A weakling! A pathetic, sad human being!*"

Quietly, and with great respect, she listened to my tirade. Then she said, "Did you ask for help?"

"Help? *Help?* No, I did not ask for help! To be honest, Heather, that hadn't even occurred to me. Asking for help isn't exactly one of my strongest qualities. Who exactly would I be asking help from, may I ask?"

"John of God. The Entities.," Heather replied simply.

"Heather, not to be rude or disrespectful or anything, but honestly, I don't even know who the Entities are that you are referring to," I said in a slightly snide tone of voice.

Heather smiled as I ranted. "You know, besides John of God and the Entities, there are others here at the *pousada* who could also help you," she suggested, kindly.

I got a little snippy then. "You mean like humans? Like the other guests? Heather, everyone else staying here right now can do whatever they want, but I'm stuck here in this room. I can't even go outside because the light hurts my eyes. I have to say, this isn't exactly a vacation, now is it? I have absolutely nothing to distract me! I am seriously not having any fun at all right now."

"That's probably exactly how John of God and the Entities want it to be for you right now."

"Well, it sucks." I pouted.

We talked for a while longer and then Heather asked me a question that would change the course of my life: "Did you know it is a spiritual law that God, John of God, the Entities, or any other Being of Light cannot intervene or help in your life unless you invite them to do so?"

"No, I did not know that," I answered, honestly.

"You might wish to consider that, you know, as long as you are struggling with all these questions."

"But," I cried, as tears welled up, "I *never* ask for help! I stopped asking for help when I was little. I learned very early that I had to be strong and know how to take care of myself. I already told you I don't know *how* to ask for help! Don't you get it?" Tears were streaming down my face.

"Well, it is my understanding and experience that it's a Cosmic Law that you must *ask* for help. Those who wait to help us, any time of our day or night, cannot intervene without *an actual request* from us. Mary Anne, you have to actually, literally ask for help *before* They can help you."

"Oh yeah *right*!" I was now screaming. "Ask for help. From *whom*? *Who* exactly am I talking to? This is *all* so crazy Heather! *Ask* for *help*. Are you *kidding* me? This is *all* a total *waste* of my *time*!" I was practically snarling at her.

Heather just sat there across from me on the other double bed and smiled calmly. I guess she had seen other people come unglued before. She said, Well, I think that for everyone, it is a little different. Some people pray or talk with their conception of God when they ask for help on whatever issue it is that they are struggling with. Many people here talk with John of God or the Spiritual Entities who work with him at the Casa when they need help, healing, or assistance. I really don't think it matters. What matters is that you ask for help. And then, in my experience, help a*lways* comes.

"Are you absolutely, positively *sure* of that? About help *always* coming if you ask?" I was calming down a little now and wiping my tears with the end of my T-shirt.

"Yes, Mary Anne. I am absolutely sure of it." Heather held my gaze and I knew she was serious and also that she spoke from experience. Then she added, "It's worth a try at least." She smiled and then she got up and left my room. I was alone again. I sat there on my bed for quite a while, replaying our exchange over in my mind. It was obvious that what I had been doing up to this point was not working. I figured I had nothing to lose in asking for just a little help. As she had said, it was worth a try at least.

I lay down and closed my eyes. "Ahem. Entities? God? Angels? Whoever you are, will you please help me figure out what I need to understand about why I am here? *Please help me* understand why I chose to come all the way to Brazil to see John of God. And can you also please help me understand what really, really needs to be healed within me and my life? Right now, my heart just feels like a geode, absolutely impossible to crack open, and I don't know what to do. *Please help me.*"

As soon as I finished saying '*Please help me,*' inner visions and dreams began in my mind's eye. It was like someone had just popped in a DVD and my life was on it. I saw a long line of people all standing in line to my left, exactly like those who waited to be seen by John of God at the Casa. Each person, some of whom I recognized immediately and some I did not, stood there waiting patiently. I had the intuition that it somehow was my job to usher them in one by one and see what they wanted from me. It felt as if, in some strange way, I needed to forgive them.

The first person in line was someone I knew well, and my first instinct was to tell him, "There is no way I am ever going to forgive *you*." He smiled politely and said, "Fine. I'll just get back into line, then." He turned around and started walking back to the end of the line.

It was clear that he was coming back eventually. I understood then that I was going to have to face him eventually, and that this exercise—or whatever it was—was certainly was not going to be easy. I could "see" that there were a lot of people in line, and I was mad at them *all.*

I tried to understand what I was supposed to be doing, and as I faced each person in turn, it seemed that not only did I have to see, from my own perspective, why I was angry at them, but I also needed to look at the situation from their perspective. As I looked back at myself, from their perspective, I suddenly understood that they were totally justified in their feelings of anger toward me for how they perceived what I had done to them.

Only in the moment when I saw things from both sides, completely equally, did I understand that the exchange between us was "completed."

Then, as soon as each exchange was complete, and I could completely see the situation from both of our perspectives, the person facing me turned rather misty, and instantly they dissolved in a whirling motion into nothingness. This went on for several days, as I figured out, person by person, who and what I needed to forgive, and what I needed to understand about each relationship. As the days went by, and more people dissolved, the line got shorter, too.

One after the other, I did see things from both sides, and one after the other, I was able to forgive and forgive and forgive. The two huge, unbearably heavy sacks of rotten rage and resentment "potatoes" I had been carrying around on my back all of my life kept getting lighter and lighter.

Finally, there was only one person left, the same person I had sent back over and over again. And finally I was able to see both of our points of view, and then he, too, dissolved, just like all the others.

Eight days later, I was to go back to see John of God for a follow-up "check-up,", just as I would with my regular doctor. As I got closer to him, I began to cry again because I felt it was such a loving and protected space. John of God took my hand as I kneeled, and it appeared to me that he smiled and tilted his head toward me slightly, as if to say, *You certainly did your work, now didn't you?*

Heather translated for him my same question as before, since I still was not clear on the answer: "With all my gifts and talents, where do I serve God best?" And he sent me on into the current, to be near him as I sat in meditation. After eight days of doing all that forgiveness work, I had no idea what to expect. I sat down, closed my eyes, and patiently waited. Then, all of a sudden, the inner DVD started again in my mind, but with a different story.

This time, were three "doors" appeared in my inner field of vision. The doors opened one, two, three. Behind door number one, I saw myself accepting an Academy Award. Behind door number two, I saw myself in the Oval Office, helping the president of the United States. Behind door number three, I saw myself in the grocery line at the grocery store, speaking with the grocery store clerk.

And inside my head, I heard the words, *"What do these three pictures have in common?"*

I looked at the doors and thought, *I really do not know. Really, I don't.*

Then the Voice of my Inner Wisdom said, *"It doesn't really matter where you are or what you are doing. You can be at the Academy Awards, the Oval Office, or the grocery store. It isn't your brilliant technique that is the most healing for your clients or the people around you, you know."*

What!? I thought. *Not my technique? Hey, I have worked on that technique for years now.*

"Nope," this Voice of my Inner Wisdom said. *"Mary Anne, you must learn that it is the power of your presence that is healing. Just your energy coming into a room or in close connection to a person brings with it healing energy that they feel and feel healed from."*

I honestly found this very hard to believe, as if this Voice of my Inner Wisdom was talking about someone else. Then those three doors closed rapidly and another three came into view. The Voice of my Inner Wisdom said, *"Now we'd like to show you who you really are. Ready?"*

"I think so."

And then the three doors opened, and I saw one scene after the other. I saw times when I had shared a kind word with a homeless person or given someone something that no one else but the two of us would ever know about. I saw myself being kind to people, affirming, and I saw my heartfelt loving, compassionate giving. I had totally forgotten most of these events, but when I looked at them on this "inner DVD," they all seemed so real, very familiar, and not long ago in time.

Then the Voice of my Inner Wisdom asked, *"So how do you feel about that woman? The Mary Anne who you see here in these pictures?"*

I heard myself respond, all choked up, *"Well, I rather like her. In fact, I love her."*

Then the Voice of my Inner Wisdom said, *"Yes. That is the entire point. Love. Loving who you truly are. Now you will finally know what it is to truly thrive. You will thrive no matter what the circumstances or events are at any given moment."*

I found myself nodding in amazement. Then my Inner Wisdom said to me, *"So how do you feel, right now, at this moment?"*

I stopped, thought for a moment and then said, *"I feel p-p-p-peaceful?"*

At that moment, it felt like the bottom of my chair fell out and I was transported to this beautiful, colorful space of peace and love and calm. All I can say is I was not truly conscious for I do not know how long. It felt like my entire internal compass was being reset. It was as if I finally knew what "True North" was in my deepest being and essence. I stayed there in that place of complete peace until I heard, almost from far away, the "Hail Mary, full of grace" from the room, and it was time to get up.

I left Brazil and the Casa with a deep feeling of gratitude for all that I had experienced and learned. It was a soulful journey I would never forget and it felt as if it would transform my future life forever. I was not at all sure about how that future would manifest, but I felt sure that it would be exactly what I needed to become who I was meant to be.

My heart no longer felt like a geode. My transformation was complete. In my final meeting with John of God, just before I left the Casa, I asked if he could please help me get my book written and published. He smiled, squeezed my hand, and nodded.

From Me
To You...

Visiting John of God isn't something that everyone can or will do in their lifetimes. But everyone can have an experience of transformation that is just as powerful. Ask for help and it will come. Open yourself up and see what you find. Sometimes when you crack open, that's the only way the Light of Transformation can get in.

Heather Cummings' book is entitled: *John of God: The Healer Who Has Transformed Millions.*

Peace

In a Perfect World

The concept of peace has been debated, fought over, and meditated on all around the world for centuries. In fact, if you were to ask me right now what I most longed for, I would answer without hesitation: peace. I would suspect that my relentless pursuit of perfection has something to do with why I don't feel peaceful a lot of the time. But I really think there is much more to a lack of peace than just a self-sabotaging pursuit of perfection. So why is peace so difficult for most of us to achieve, on a moment-to-moment basis?

Our world has become increasingly complex. Information in the world is now doubling every two to three years and is soon expected to double every year. Just the fact that all this information is at our fingertips, through our computers and phones at any time, and our access is only limited to how fast we can type, it's no wonder we are stressed out.

In a political sense, peace is complex. The American rock guitarist, composer and singer Jimi Hendrix said, "When the power of love overcomes the love of power, the world will know peace." The Indian philosopher Mahatma Gandhi, well-known and respected for his doctrine of non-violent protest, suggested, "Each one has to find peace from within. And peace, to be real, must be unaffected by outside circumstances." Sometimes I find it hard to love, and at times, outside circumstances really get to me. Then my peace within is totally shot.

So where is peace hidden in all of this chaos and politics? One of my favorite poets, Rumi, described peace in this way: "Out beyond ideas of wrong doing and right doing, there is a field. I'll meet you there." Many times I have wished that the people of this world could just figure out how to meet in that field Rumi speaks of. Perhaps if we did, together we could all find peace and just get along. In the meantime, I'm working on trying to find that non-violent, peaceful field, right here in my own mind and heart.

I know that I get closest to true peace in my meditations when I sit and rest in the quiet of both my spirit and my faith. I also know peace when I walk in the sand along the ocean or gaze out over the water from my window. And perhaps, those little bits of peace are the best I can do for now, when I am also raising my kids, running my business, and trying to be a good and loyal friend. But I like to think that peace is always available to me at any time, within, and that peace is always as close as my own breath.

Babbie Mason and Cheryl Rogers wrote a beautiful song, entitled "In a Perfect World," that really expresses what I would wish for each of us as we slowly work our way toward a full understanding and experience of peace. Here are some excerpts from that beautiful song:

"A heart that never fears, can you imagine that?
And the only tears we weep, are tears of joy.
Every hunger satisfied and every baby's cry would be heard.
A soul that never grieves, can you imagine that?
The darkness that has no power.
No desperate lonely hours, to make it through until the morning light.
And we would see the hope in each sunrise....

In a perfect world, there would always be a second chance allowed.
In a perfect world, there would be enough love to go around, somehow.
And peace would be the sweetest sound on earth, in a perfect world.

A faith with wings to fly, can you imagine that?
And the will to try is never far away.
Every man would know his Call.
And something in us all, would long to see a wounded spirit heal.
And live to see our brother's dream fulfilled.

In a perfect world, there would always be a second chance allowed.
In a perfect world, there would be enough love to go around, somehow.
And peace would be the sweetest sound on earth, in a perfect world."

—Babbie Mason and Cheryl Rogers, "In a Perfect World", Grateful Bread Music (ICG), Gaither Copyright Management (ASCAP)

From Me
To You...

My obstacle towards attaining personal peace is my relentless pursuit of perfection. What's yours?

Leora Cashe does a wonderful cover of "In a Perfect World," which you can find on her CD, *Inspiration*. And while you're listening to *Inspiration*, check out her cover of "Hallelujahs," by Chris Rice. It's incredibly beautiful and moving.

Judgment

A Close Call

One day my son Joshua, age fourteen, announced that he had decided to ride the STP, a 202–mile cycling race from Seattle to Portland, all in one day. I thought he was kidding.

I knew nothing about the STP or road bikes, so I called our dear friends, Ali and Marianne, both experienced cyclists, and asked them what they thought. Both of them had ridden the STP ride and completed it in one day. Without hesitation, they both said, "If he wants to do it, we think he should try." I felt very hesitant and said, "But he has very little 'time in the saddle' training on his new road bike. Will he even make it?"

Ali smiled and said, "Well hey, what's he doing this weekend? I could take him out with some other male riders I know who would be on the STP ride he wants to do. It's called the Death Ride, and many cyclists use it as a warm-up for the STP. We could see how he does on the Death Ride and then go from there in terms of his training. It will also give him a clue about what he is getting into and what the STP ride will be like."

"The Death Ride? It's actually called the Death Ride, Ali? Are you sure that's such a good idea?" I asked, looking back and forth between Ali's and Marianne's faces. They were both grinning, but their eyes were serious.

"Sure. He'd better know what he's getting himself into. If he can't get through the Death Ride, he sure won't be able to get through the STP. Also, there will be lots of riders in our group who could look him over and speak their minds about whether he's really capable or not. Plus, he will learn a lot from these really experienced riders, even if he decides ultimately not to do the STP with us. But, in the end, you are his mother, and it really is up to you whether to let him go or not."

I thought for a moment. It sure sounded like it couldn't hurt to give Joshua a better idea of what he was getting himself into. "Let's do it!" I said, with a hesitant smile.

Joshua went out on the Death Ride, and afterward the verdict from the other riders was split. Some in the group wondered if Ali was out of his mind to even bring Joshua on the Death Ride with so little training ahead of time. These riders absolutely said Joshua was not ready for the STP, and should have started training six months earlier, like everyone else.

Ali, ever the optimist, said, "Joshua did great. I was really proud of him. He stuck with it when others might have quit. He's got a lot of guts for a kid that age. I think he should try the STP. Steve and I will stick close to him, ride with him and help see him through."

Marianne added, "And I have volunteered to be the 'sag wagon' this year, and you can ride along with me, if you want." I soon learned that the "sag wagon" is the van that follows behind STP riders of all shapes and sizes with support, food, and encouragement. I was happy to go just to keep an eye on Joshua, so I could be sure he would be safe.

I had to admit that while Joshua had waited until very late in the game to get ready for the STP race, he certainly had the courage, guts, and determination to try it. I had as much support as possible lined up for him and could also keep an eye on him along the way. He had a new dream and focus. I really wanted to support him in this new direction. A real adventure was shaping up!

The riders all left Seattle at 5 a.m. About four in the afternoon, at mile 197 (with just five miles left in the race), Joshua "hit the wall" of exhaustion and began to wobble on his bike. After traveling at an average of 17.3 miles per hour for eleven hours with only a few breaks, Joshua nearly wobbled into an oncoming truck. We pulled him off the road and into a parking lot.

The other riders huddled together and had a conference about Joshua's safety—and their own safety riding with him. How risky was it to let Joshua continue? While they debated in a circle at the other end of the parking lot, I sat with Joshua as he lay on the grass with his feet up on the trunk of a tree. I handed him an electrolyte drink. He could barely hold it so I took it back, opened it and helped him get the drink down his throat.

After we got some of the drink down, I took the bottle back so it wouldn't get tipped over and then asked him, "So, Joshua. How are you? Really?"

From his prone position on the ground, and too tired to even hold his drink, Joshua turned his head slowly to the right to look at me, but didn't say anything. He was quite dazed, and looked like a boxer who had just been hit with a blistering right hook. He was pale and his eyes were out of focus. He just lay there: quiet and still, staring at me, but almost as if he did not recognize who I was. This scared me.

"Joshua? Can you hear me?"

After a few more moments, Joshua choked out sarcastically, "Yeah, Mom, I can hear you. And yeah, I think it's pretty obvious that I'm exhausted, Mom."

"Yeah, Joshua, I hear that." After getting up at 3 a.m. to get him to Ali and Marianne's by 4 a.m., and following him for 197 miles in a hot van, I was getting tired myself. "I and everyone else here are really trying to help you."

"Oh, yeah. Sorry, Mom."

"It's okay," I sighed. *What is the best thing to do here?* I kept asking myself over and over again inside my head.

Then Joshua suddenly spoke, "I'm just *so mad*. I've quit *so* many things in my life that I shouldn't have. I'm *so* close now on this that if I don't finish, I'll never forgive myself."

I shook my head. "This has nothing to do with forgiving yourself. We all want you to be safe and not cause yourself or anyone else harm. And we are all trying to make the best judgment call we can. Quite frankly, right this moment, as your mother, I do not know what the right judgment call is. I really don't."

Joshua sat up and held out his hand for the electrolyte drink. He began to gulp it down.

"Hey, don't drink that too fast or you might end up getting sick."

"Oh, yeah, right. Thanks," Joshua said as he slowed down and his eyes began to come back into focus.

"Listen, Joshua, you are young and can always ride another year. We just don't want anything bad to happen to you. That's what they are all discussing over there, basically, whether to let you continue."

Joshua suddenly perked up and his eyes flashed red. It was as if someone had given him a shot of adrenaline. I realized this was in part due to the electrolyte drink the other riders had told me to get down his throat any way I could.

"Joshua, help me understand. Why is this race, and doing it in one day, so important to you?"

Suddenly, Joshua burst out into a rage:

"Look, I'm *not* quitting now, Mom. I've quit *so* many things right before I finished them. What do I have, five miles left to go? Look, this is my dream to do this, not anybody else's, OK? I don't care what any of you say. I'm *not quitting*. I've come all this way and I'm *not* giving up. I'll ride by myself if I have to!"

He started to get up, then got wobbly and dizzy and sat back down again on the grass, still holding on to the tree trunk.

I shook my head. "Well, I'm just going to have to put my foot down on this one. None of us can let you continue if you can't walk. Your safety is the most important thing. If you are going to be losing control of your bike and riding into oncoming traffic, we just can't let you continue. I'm sorry."

"Yeah. OK, Mom. I get that."

"But, Joshua, I will say this, and please listen to me very carefully, now. It is my firm belief that the truly wise part of you, the deep part of you that started this whole race thing, knows how to finish it."

"Thanks, Mom," Joshua said, as he used the tree to pull himself up to a standing position.

"OK, here's the deal," I said, speaking from a deeper, more spiritual place of judgment. "I believe in the part of you that has this dream. I *believe* in that deeper part of you that knows how to finish this. So I am going to say, as your mother and your witness: *Go* for it."

"Really, Mom? You think I can make it?" Suddenly he looked terribly frightened.

"Yes. I believe in you and your spirit that started this whole thing. Just promise me one thing, will you?"

"What is it, Mom?"

"If you think you are going to fall or need to take a break in these last few miles, you will use your best judgment to do what is most safe. I don't want to lose you, here at the end."

"Thanks for believing in me, Mom."

"I always have and I always will. You will see me at the end cheering for you when you cross over the finish line."

As I watched him pull out of that strip-mall parking lot just past the last rest stop, milepost 197, with Ali and Steve flanking him in case he just fell over, I felt this grip on my heart, and I prayed for God to please watch over them all.

It was only later that night that Ali and Steve told me what Joshua said after they had pulled out of that strip-mall parking lot and were out of eyesight of Marianne and I: "Ali and Steve, I'm scared. I know this was my dream. But I'm not sure I can make it."

At that moment, both Ali and Steve smiled great smiles of courage to Joshua. Steve said, "Well, Josh, Ali and I just want you to know that this isn't up to you anymore. You are going to make it to the end of this race. Even if we two have to personally *drag* you over the finish line, you are going to *finish* this race!"

They told me that at that moment, Joshua smiled a devilish smile, turned to Ali, and with a twinkle in his eye, said, "Hey, Ali! Let's step it up a notch, shall we?" And then he took off. Joshua never looked back until he had crossed the finish line, five miles later. He had made his dream to ride the STP in one day, at age fourteen, a reality.

Now, looking back on it, I can see that this race against himself was a pivotal moment in his life. Joshua's unique determination really seemed to accelerate after the STP, when he finished something huge that he had set his mind to. It also served him over and over, and especially four years later when, at age eighteen, he decided to take a solo backpacking trip through the Middle East.

That was another time when, even though my personal judgment said it was not such a good idea, it was his judgment and belief in himself that I had to trust. And just as with the STP, his trip to the Middle East continued to develop his sense of belief in himself and his judgment. In each case, he tested his own perceived limits and won, though it could have just as easily turned the other way on him. No matter what I said or felt, ultimately it was Joshua alone who had to discover what he was capable of, and I, as his parent, had to wait for him at the finish line.

From Me
To You...

Have you judged a part of yourself or your life too harshly? Has your judgment been: "This isn't possible," "I can't do that," or "I'm not good (strong, brave, smart) enough?" If so, perhaps you can turn your judgment to a more positive direction and take a courageous leap to try something you may have always felt was out of your reach. As Henry David Thoreau said, "If you build your sandcastles in the air, you need not be lost. Now put the foundations under them."

So if you have built a "sandcastle" of something totally new in your life, what is your next best step?

If you don't have a dream to aspire to right now, why not create one?

Power

Don't Leave Home without It

So often the people I talk with say they feel powerless: powerless to change themselves, others, their circumstances, their life. I certainly share a sense of feeling powerless at times. I have learned, that often when we feel we are most powerless, we are in fact at our most powerful.

There is something quite powerful that takes over inside us when we absolutely know we are right and we know the other person knows it, too. We don't always get our way, even if we are right, and others may still refuse to do the right thing, in the end. But to be a witness to ourselves or to someone who stands firm in his or her own belief is inspiring.

Observing someone who stands firmly in the power of his or her faith and country can be equally breathtaking. Recently, National Public Radio aired a story about a Muslim woman who had been a translator for the Allies in World War II. Normally, translators in that job lasted a week before the Nazis found them and tortured them to give up information. This woman lasted three months in the job, and when the Nazis captured her and tortured her, they could never break her.

Her captors themselves began to doubt that they even had the right woman. Her internal power, her Muslim faith, and her belief in what was right for a better world, were far too strong to allow any physical torture to shake them.

There are all kinds of ways that healthy power shows up in the world.

When my daughter, Sarah, was two and a half years old, she nearly drowned. But it was the power of music that brought her back to life.

Before she was born, Sarah's dad and I participated in a program at Cedars Sinai Hospital in Los Angeles called "The Womb Song" project. Doctors were trying to determine at what age in the womb babies could actually hear and also when they would begin to have memory.

Each parent was instructed to come up with a sixteen-bar song that would equal a total of one minute of singing. This Womb Song was then recorded and put onto a loop tape. Both the mother's and father's songs were then played for the child *in utero* in twenty-minute sessions, two times a day, for total of eight weeks.

These are the words of my Womb Song for Sarah:

"Oh, Angel Baby, I never knew
I could never love anyone as I love you.
You are the sunshine that brightens my days.
Oh, Angel Baby, I'll love you always."

When Sarah was a tiny baby, I would sing this song to her to calm her whenever she struggled with croup. If she was colicky, it would calm her, too. Gradually, when she could talk, she learned the Womb Song, and we would sing it together.

When Sarah was two and a half, we were in Tahoe at a swimming pool. I was at the foot of the pool stairs and Sarah stepped into the swimming pool and slipped. She hit her head on the railing and then fell face down into the water. I immediately scooped her up and carried her out of the pool. But she had already inhaled enough water to stop her breathing. I panicked and screamed for someone to call 911.

As I was holding her, I watched her gradually turn blue. I did not know CPR. As the blue color reached her ears, all I could think of was to start singing her Womb Song. It was like calling someone back from the dead. Her head jerked forward, she spit out an amazing amount of water, and then started trying to sing along with me. When the paramedics arrived, they told me it was a miracle that she was alive. I knew it was a miracle and the power of music.

Now Sarah has gone on into a career in singing and musical theater. Her voice and presence on stage are powerful and vulnerable at the same time.

I sang her Womb Song to her just the other day. When she heard it, she smiled and then shook her head like she was clearing cobwebs.

Photo by: Lauren Hartman

Sarah said that she had a weird and vague recollection of that song from somewhere deep within her. When I told her the story again of the Womb Song and her near-drowning, she said she was so grateful to be alive and to have had such a good life so far. I was so glad a part of her had remembered her song, the powerful song that had saved her life so long ago.

From Me
To You...

Check out my blog for another inspiring story of Power:
www.WordsToThriveBy.com

Mary Anne's Lucky Twenty-One Power Playlist:

1. Unwritten
   Natasha Bedingfield, *Unwritten*

2. Good Love Is on the Way
   John Mayer, *The Village Sessions*

3. Fall
   Peter Mayer, *Million Year Mind*

4. Firework
   Katy Perry, *Teenage Dream*

5. It's Growing
   James Taylor, *Covers*

6. Beauty in the World
   Macy Gray, *The Sellout*

7. You and Me
   Dave Matthews Band, *Big Whiskey and the GrooGrux King*

8. The Luckiest
   Ben Folds, *Rockin' the Suburbs*

9. One of These Things First
   Nick Drake, *Way to Blue: An Introduction to Nick Drake Singer/Songwriter*

10. Live Like We're Dying
    Kris Allen, *Kris Allen iTunes Pass*

11. Ready to Love Again
    Lady Antebellum, *Need You Now*

12. The Man in the Mirror
    Michael Jackson, *Michael Jackson's Vision*

13. Get off of My Cloud
    Rolling Stones, *Hot Rocks 1964–1971*

14. One
    Eleisha Eagle, *Lamplighter*

15. True Colors
    Cyndi Lauper, *The Essential Cyndi Lauper*

16. Rise
    Eddie Vedder, *Into the Wild (Music for the Motion Picture)*

17. Born This Way
    Lady Gaga, *Born This Way*

18. Amazing
    One eskimO, *One eskimO*

19. Stuck Like Glue
    Sugarland, *Stuck Like Glue*

20. Brand New Day
    Sting, *The Very Best of Sting & The Police*

21. Work It Out
    Jurassic 5 & Dave Matthews Band, *Feedback*

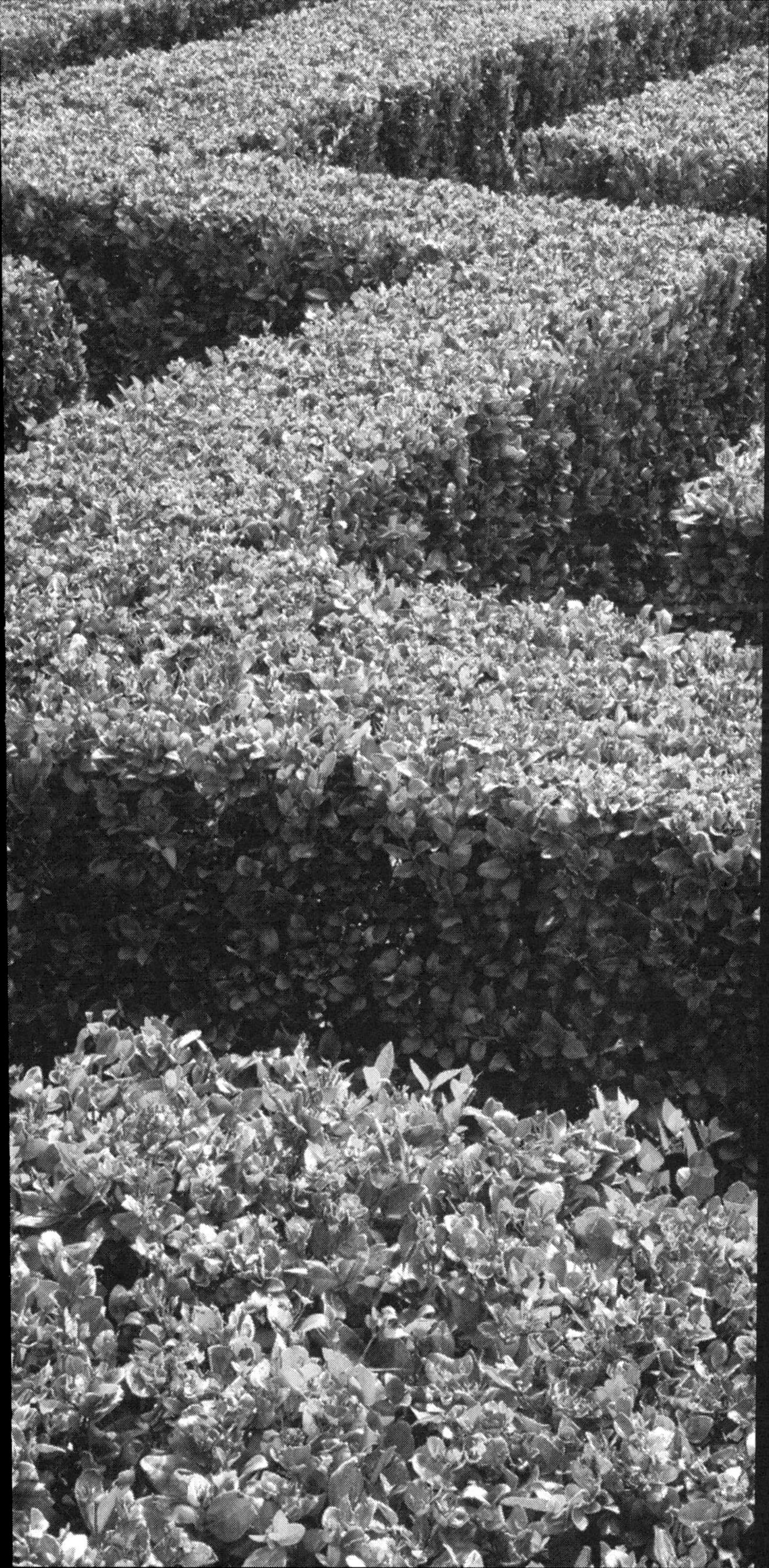

When I was recovering from cancer, I went to a wonderful healing retreat center called Harmony Hill, on Hood Canal in Washington. It was an amazing, sacred space and turned out to be exactly what I needed.

While I was there, I was quite drawn to one of the two labyrinths on the property. As I walked the labyrinth one day, I was feeling particularly agitated and uncomfortable. There was a lot going on in my life, and I had a lot of conflicting feelings at the time.

At lunch, Gretchen, Harmony Hill's founder, told me the story of the powerful and healing giant cedar tree in the middle of the labyrinth. After a brief history of the labyrinth, Gretchen also told me that they had named the tree: "She Who Knows."

So after lunch, I decided to walk the labyrinth again and have a little chat with She Who Knows.

When I finally got to the center of the labyrinth, I leaned my head and body into She Who Knows. I spread my arms wide to embrace this magnificent cedar tree. I knew I needed help, and I had learned well during my time in Brazil that no one, not even a tree spirit, could intervene in my life without my actually *asking* for help. I had also been told that *help always comes*. So with my eyes closed, my forehead resting on the bark of the tree, and my arms open wide hugging this giant tree, I mentally asked for help:

I don't know what to do. I can't see clearly. Please help me.

Almost immediately, I had these words flashed into my head: *"Be at peace with change."*

There certainly had been a lot of change in my life. And I was getting better at handling it, but I certainly wasn't at my best right then.

"Be at peace with change," I heard again in my head.

I wondered: was I really at peace with change, or was I still resistant to it? Hadn't resistance been at the core of most of my distress? How exactly does a person become at peace with change?

"Be at peace with change," I heard a third time, and at that moment, the dinner bell rang, as if punctuating the message.

As I left the labyrinth and walked to another delicious vegetarian dinner inside the lodge, I thought about what being at peace with change really meant. The only constant in the world is change. So if we fight that flow of change, then we are fighting the flow of life itself. In fact, to fight change is to cause distress in our lives. But to let the changes flow is to allow everything to be exactly what and how it is, and this includes people as much as it does our circumstances. This practice of non-resistance is at the core of what allows us to be and remain at peace.

As I was drifting off to sleep in my cozy bed that night, I thought, *"Be at peace with change,"* seemed to be at the core of everything I had ever wanted to create in my life. In fact, it was all I ever needed to be whole.

From Me To You...

If you or someone you love is facing the challenges of cancer, here is the link to Harmony Hill:

www.harmonyhill.org

All services, meals and classes are free to both cancer patients and their caregivers. It is a truly wonderful place with an amazing staff dedicated to helping you find whatever healing you and your caretakers are seeking.

Dream

Le Rayon Vert

Every summer when I was very young, we spent the month of August in Carmel-by-the-Sea, California. Every night, at sunset, we would all sit out on the deck to watch the sun go down. We were all hoping to see "the green flash." I never really knew if the green flash was an actual reality, but it gave me something to hope for at the end of every day.

The green flash, which is seen as the sun dips below the horizon, was thought by most people to be the stuff of fables. Jules Verne brought this phenomenon to public attention in his 1882 novel *Le Rayon Vert* (The Green Ray). He described "a green which no artist could ever obtain on his palette, a green of which neither the varied tints of vegetation nor the shades of the most limpid sea could ever produce the like! If there is a green in Paradise, it cannot be but of this shade, which most surely is the true green of Hope." I wondered, how did Jules Verne ever learned of the sunset flash in the first place. He was an avid sailor, so maybe he picked up the reference from a seaman or on one of his own voyages.

In an editorial in *Monthly Weather Review* 33, 408 (1905), there is the statement that "...the green ray seen just as the last glimpse of the sun disappears below the sea horizon was originally introduced into meteorology by Tyndall as an evidence of the special absorptive power of the aqueous vapor in the lowest layer of the atmosphere."

So even without knowing these literary or scientific references, every sunset of my life, from the time I was three or four years old, I watched the sun cross the horizon line just in case today would be the day that the green flash would happen. And every sunset, when it didn't happen, I would feel just a little let down.

When I was forty-seven, I took a cruise on a sailboat. One night, in the middle of the Atlantic Ocean, heading from Morocco toward Portugal, I was standing at the front of the boat at sunset as I always did, hoping for the green flash. Waiting. Waiting. Waiting.

I noticed a man, who looked about ninety years old, standing behind me to my left. He seemed to be waiting for something, too, though perhaps he was just taking in the beautiful water view and the sight of the amazing red dust swirling up from the deserts of Africa.

I turned around and said cheerfully with a laugh, "Hi. Well it looks like it's just the two of us out here. Are you waiting for the fabled green flash at sunset, too?"

"As a matter of fact, I am," he replied with a grin.

I was delighted. "Have you ever seen it?" I asked hopefully. "I have been waiting to see it for forty-four years, ever since I was three or four. Never seen it yet. Honestly, I'm beginning to think it's a myth."

Photo courtesy of www.hollandamerica.com

He laughed. "I certainly can understand you wondering if it is a myth. If it's any comfort to you, dear, I have been waiting eighty-five years to see it myself, ever since I was five years old. Perhaps we will bring each other luck tonight!" He grinned, and that blooming smile on his face and the twinkle in his eye made him look like a man half his age.

At that moment, we had just rounded the farthest southwest tip of Europe, called Cabo de Sao Vicente, off the southern tip of Portugal. In the Middle Ages, this windblown cape was believed to be the end of the world. The Romans called it the Promontorium Sacrum (Sacred Promontory). For even longer in time, this place has had religious associations, including the legend that in the fourth century, Saint Vincent's body washed ashore here from God-only-knows-where.

Today, with its 200-foot cliffs fronting the Atlantic, it still presents an awe-inspiring sight. The ocean waves have created long, sandy beaches and carved deep caves into the cliffs. Since the fifteenth century, Cabo Sao Vicente has been an important reference point for shipping, and the present lighthouse is said to be the most powerful in Europe.

Suddenly my new friend and I heard the captain announce over the loud speaker, "Folks, this is the most unusually clear day any of us have seen over the Atlantic in decades. You might want to stop whatever you are doing and come out on deck and see the sunset tonight. It will be spectacular."

I turned to my companion and smiled. Without saying a word, we locked eyes and raised our eyebrows simultaneously. We already knew that in order to see the green flash, the horizon had to be absolutely free from atmospheric interference, clouds or haze. This could be the day. It was crisp; the wind was up, the horizon clear.

Soon, people began pouring onto the deck of the Wind Spirit, our four-masted sailing yacht.

The sun went down, bit by bit…down and down…with all of us silently facing it. As the sun drew lower to the horizon line, the crew began to come out on deck too. Everyone—about 150 people—was now shoulder-to-shoulder, passenger and crew alike all facing the horizon line. All hands were truly on deck.

Just as the sun passed the extraordinarily clear horizon line, a collective gasp rose from the group. There it was, in all its amazing, green glory: a color somewhere between absinthe and shining emeralds blooming up from the horizon, just where the ball of bright yellow sun had gone down. It lasted about two to three seconds and with a flash, it was gone.

There was a moment more of silence, and then I turned to my ninety-year-old friend and started literally jumping up and down, shouting, "Did you *see* that? Did you *see* that? Oh my God! I *saw* it!! I saw the green flash! *Finally* after *all* these years I saw it! It isn't a myth after all!!!!"

He was so excited he started jumping up and down, too, and was saying, "Oh my, I have been waiting eighty-five years of my life for this moment! I can die in peace now!!! *Wow*! We did it! *The green flash*!"

Our excitement was palpable and infectious: crew and guests alike all started jumping up and down, saying how *amazing* this was and what a *night* for such a *cool* thing to happen. It really was a shared moment of exultation and joy. (And I thought that riding a camel for the first time in Morocco that morning had been the highlight of my day!) I had seen one lifelong dream come true right before my eyes. I suddenly felt an overwhelming sense of hope, grace, and gratitude.

In my cabin that night after dinner, I got to thinking that this green flash was only one of many dreams of my life. Now that this one was fulfilled, what would I focus on next? There were many dreams I had been pondering, but had not yet acted on. There were also dreams I had given up on at that point, just because they seemed impossible. And there were other dreams I still believed in that had not yet come true.

I also thought about how, if I had I given up on the green flash and become bitter after all those years of disappointment, I might have stayed at the pool and missed it that day on the boat. I could have told myself, *Oh, so what? Every other time I have been wrong and it never happened. Why should this day be any different? Stop hoping. It's probably a myth anyway.*

But I had not given up hope. There is something remarkable about human beings' capacity in this area. We have the capacity to believe—even in things, people, events, as yet unseen that aren't guaranteed. I truly believe that if you can dream it, you can create it. Somewhere within you absolutely knows how or where to go to take the next best step forward toward achieving your dreams.

And that night, seeing the green flash out on the Atlantic after forty-four years of waiting, was truly one of the absolute highlights of my life. It was a dream definitely worth waiting for!

From Me
To You...

For more information on the green flash, you can do an Internet search on Google. Simply type in "green flash." You will find some amazing links to photos of the green flash, as well as more background information in Wikipedia.

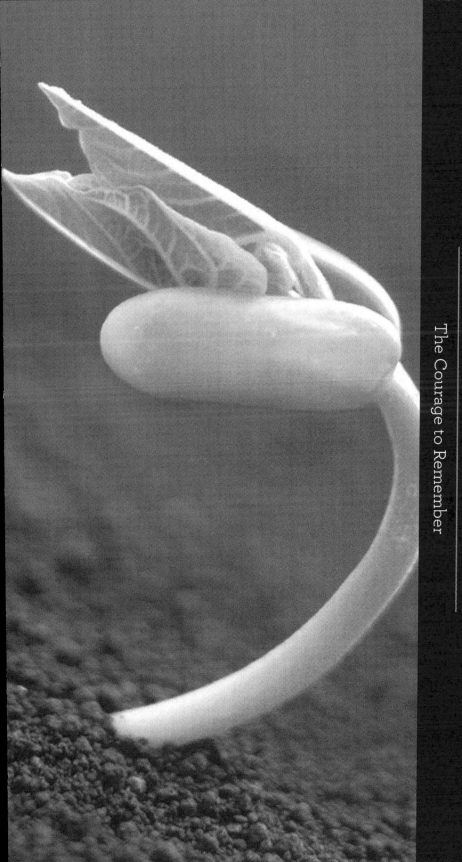

The Courage to Remember

One day, out of the blue, I received a phone call from an old classmate named Randy whom I had not spoken to since second grade. We got to catching up, and Randy told me this story:

"I sat behind you for all of second grade. And one day you drew this picture of a boy and a girl holding hands. Under the boy's picture you wrote 'Randy' and under the girl's picture you wrote, 'Mary Anne.' I remember that you turned around to show me your picture and you had such a happy, bright face. I'm embarrassed to admit that I proceeded to slaughter you. In my defense I was only a boy of, what, eight? Well, even that is not a very good defense, and I am really sorry I did that to you. But anyway, truth be told, I made fun of you. I told you your drawing was stupid. I teased you mercilessly at recess. You never said a word. But your face I will never forget as long as I live.

"When we came back from recess, you went to your desk, picked up the picture you had drawn of us. With your eyes locked on mine and with the saddest face I have ever seen in my life, you crumpled your drawing of us up into a tight little ball. Then you turned away from me, walked over to the other side of the room, and threw the ball of paper really hard right into the trash can.

"Then you burst into tears. You walked back to your desk and refused to ever turn around to talk to me for the rest of the year. I have never forgotten it all these thirty-seven years. I was so stupid. I am so sorry."

I had no recollection whatsoever of this event.

After telling Randy he didn't need to worry about this incident from our past anymore, I hung up the phone. I began thinking about what a tremendous gift this story from second grade was. Randy showed me a glimpse of myself as a very young girl, a girl who was full of resilience and strength. The more I thought about it, I felt this younger me was a me I could really admire and be proud of.

This story showed me that, at one time in my life, I had such a sense of self-worth that I would not allow another person to treat me unkindly or unfairly. That drawing, which began as my way of reaching out to share and connect with a cute boy in my class, ended up crumpled in the wastebasket as my clear message of separation from harm. My anger at his ridicule had motivated me to make this strong choice to destroy my own art.

However, even if the action was strong, the story clearly shows that my bursting into tears was a vulnerable and healthy kind of rage. My therapist told me that as long as children are not desensitized to their own feelings by abuse, they instinctively take very strong and quick actions to defend and protect themselves.

After hanging up with Randy, I sat and wondered where that part of me had gone.

In my memory as an adult, so many of my stories were about the times when I allowed other people to override my own instincts or intuition, to "walk all over me." It seemed that mostly I could remember only the times I had been

silent or not fought back when I should have. I had learned very well how to swallow my rage, my pride, my opinions and my strength. It's no wonder I had become so angry.

With the help of very good therapists and loving friends, I have worked myself through much of my self-destructive behavior. It has been a process of learning to love who I really am, stripping away the layers upon layers of untruths that others have told me, negative things that I had believed about myself for decades as if they were facts.

I am not a "bad and ungrateful child." I am not "stupid." I am not "crazy." And I sure as heck don't have "thunder thighs!"

Today, the story of myself as a young girl, full of love, openness, and righteous indignation feels so much more familiar to me. She *is* more "me" than the angry, uncertain person I had allowed myself to become. After years of sorting through my life, I have finally come full circle to who I really am: the resilient, fiery, spirited, and also thoughtful girl who I was to begin with.

Resilience is not just the ability to bounce back from anything. Resilience is, in any circumstance, the ability to be vulnerable enough to feel in the first place. It is the ability to recognize that your safety and well-being come first. And if you ever feel something is not right, or uncomfortable or dangerous, then being resilient means that you have the courage and strength to immediately remove yourself from that situation, person, or location.

There are no exceptions to this rule. None of us ever have to take care of others at our own expense. Resilience is the ability to take action on one's own behalf, even if it is hard, makes waves or is out of sync with another person. Resilience is a deep awareness of what we each need to do for ourselves to protect ourselves.

I know now that sassy, strong, tender me was never really gone. She just became a little lost. After all these years, I have made the journey home back to myself, like following the bread crumbs back to the cottage after spending so much of my life being lost in the woods. To get back to our true wholeness, we need both our vulnerability and our resilience in equal measure. This is a journey that we all must undertake eventually, even if we wait until the moment of death. It's never too late. But, why wait?

From Me
To You...

What part of the resilient, strong, and amazing you have you lost touch with? Try taking out some crayons or colored paper right now and draw a picture of that unique and resilient you. Feel free to take a photo of your drawing, including your first name and what you remembered about yourself while doing this creative exercise, and then send it to me at my blog, **www.WordsToThriveBy.com**. I will do my best to post the drawings that come in.

Trust

"Catch Me!"

If you don't test trust, then you will never find out who or what is trustworthy. You know that game people play at school or at company retreats, where you take turns falling back into another person's arms and you're told, "Don't worry, their arms are open and ready to catch you"? This game is designed as a trust-building exercise.

The test of your trust is the moment you finally release yourself, on faith, and let yourself fall.

Your trust is justified the exact moment when you know you are truly caught in the arms of the other person.

Trust, in both personal and professional life, is never a game.

Are you trusting? Are you trustworthy?

From Me
To You...

I wrote this book on faith, trusting it would find its audience.

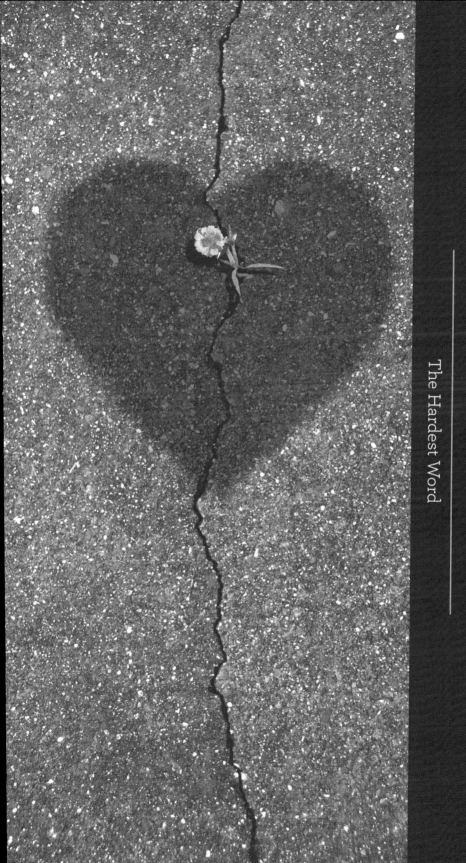

Love

The Hardest Word

I have had the hardest time of all writing about the word *love*. In fact, during the course of writing this book, I often wondered if I should just take the word *love* out, since it is a word that screws so many people up, including myself.

It became a bit spooky, actually. Every morning, I would go to my bowl that contained all the chapter word titles on slips of paper and pick one to write about that day. For weeks, every day, I kept drawing the same word: *love*.

"Oh no! Not love *again!*" I would yell to nobody in particular. "I can't do this!" And then I would very efficiently would avoid writing about it.

I left my computer and cleaned my house. I loaded and ran the dishwasher, washed my clothes, did my art homework for my class that wasn't even due for a week, went on a walk or a bike ride, talked with a neighbor, went to my mailbox, did anything but write.

As I walked or cycled, I would grumble to myself, "This word is too hard! I don't know what to say about the subject of love. How do you write about something you don't know the first thing about? This word makes everybody crazy. People have died for this word. People misuse it all the time. People say it all the time and don't mean it. It's all so confusing! I *hate* this word!" But I decided to stick it out.

I discovered that my first memories of how I viewed love were not happy ones: growing up, I used to hide in the plum tree to stay out of my father's way when he would fly into a rage. The only time I ever saw my father touch or kiss my mom was the day he left for good.

If this was "love," then I wanted nothing of it.

Later on in my life, a man asked me to marry him. At the time, I was an emotional wreck from the recent, fatal drug and alcohol overdose of my favorite brother, Bob. I believed that if I married him, this man would somehow save me from a life that felt like it was crumbling down all around me from grief.

Not long after we met, his mother, Jean, became very ill with one of the first cases of Creutzfeldt-Jakob disease ever diagnosed in the United States, and her health began to rapidly decline. As her health declined, the pain in my fiancé's family began to mount. We decided to move our wedding up six months so that hopefully his mother could be there.

A month before our wedding, just before Jean dropped into a coma, I made a spontaneous deathbed promise to her: "Please don't worry, Jean. I will always take care of your son." The moment the words came out of my mouth, I saw the tremendous relief on her face as she closed her eyes and smiled. It felt good to be able to give her some comfort.

But as we left the hospital that day, I began to have doubts. With all the grief and pain surrounding Jean's illness, and my brother's suicide, I had not had enough time to really get to know who this man was or know what I really wanted. I had not had enough time to get ready for this huge decision that would affect the rest of my life.

But I was sure of one thing: my word was my bond. I decided that no matter what, a person's word should mean something. I had given my word to his dying mother, and I would go through with the wedding.

The day of my wedding, as I rounded the bend in the church to walk down the aisle, all my feelings of conflict collided. I felt weak at the knees and close to tears. I tried not to stumble or let anything show on my face. I bravely walked to the altar, took my soon-to-be husband's hand, and said "I do."

After the wedding, I came up with a plan. I reasoned if I didn't understand love, then I could become a perfect wife, in a *Leave It to Beaver* or *The Donna Reed Show* kind of way. And I would keep my word. Over the years, I drove myself harder and harder and harder to get everything right and would punish myself if I ever made a mistake.

I became obsessive about everything. When our children were born, I vowed to do everything perfectly: baby food from scratch, Halloween costumes straight from my sewing machine, gourmet meals using homegrown produce every night, no matter what. I would be the best mother, wife, cook, dishwasher, sounding board, muse, and cocreator a person could ever wish for.

I started working harder and harder, later and later, with no rest. I was running, running, running from myself. The harder I worked, the more I ran from my feelings, the more depressed I became. As the years went on, I pushed myself to the breaking point, unable to sleep, unable to think, unable to even *remember* what went into a child's lunch, let alone make it.

This was terrifying, and I didn't know what to do or who to talk to about it. I started having panic attacks. I can remember laying down on my kitchen floor, trying to stop my heart from racing, trying to get a grip on myself. After these waves of terror and anxiety passed, I would be furious with myself for being so weak and stupid and inefficient. And then I would try to go do something mindless, like folding laundry or cooking, so I could feel productive. There was always comfort in achievement.

But at night the anxiety would start again. Would I sleep? Could I hide my insomnia, my weight loss, and my distress from my husband? I wasn't sure how long I could keep it all up. Eventually I couldn't, and my spirit broke. My grand and ultimately unrealistic plan to be the perfect wife, mother, friend, gardener, editor, brainstormer, chief cook, and bottle-washer had completely failed. I believed at that time that I had failed at my entire life and that I was utterly useless in every way.

Perfection is clearly not a bedfellow of love, but I think a lot of us get the two confused. I have learned a lot over the years about how my plan to be perfect as a substitute for love was unrealistic, unhealthy, and bound to fail. I have learned how to be more compassionate, forgiving, and yes, even loving, towards others and myself.

Sometimes it takes hitting the very bottom to snap us out of our own fantasy about who we think we are or should be, so we can finally see who we really are, what we really want and what love really is. This was certainly true for me. Love can be a revelation. I am so deeply grateful for all I learned about myself and about love from being married to my children's father. Even with all my doubts and fears at the time, I can honestly say, without a doubt, that I made the right decision to marry him. We now have children whom we both love deeply. Even through all the pain of marriage and divorce and the death of our son McKenzie, I cannot imagine my life without our thriving children, Sarah and Joshua.

Through it all, I developed the courage to open up and love both myself and others at the same time, not one to the exclusion of the other. I learned, while being married and divorced, how to improve my verbal skills, and now I am far better able to negotiate. I have gained self-confidence as I have learned how to advocate for myself toward a win-win outcome rather than a win-lose outcome, with me always putting myself on the losing side.

Learning to stand up for ourselves is challenging and hard for many of us. We want people to love us for who we really are, but we also fear being rejected. But if we are playing a role to get that love, then the people around us never really know us. They are, in fact, loving a fantasy, a mirage that could very well go up in smoke at any moment.

The first step is to learn how to love ourselves.

Loving ourselves means finally allowing ourselves to become truly vulnerable and become whole-hearted people, living in a true sense of worthiness. This vulnerability allows us to explore and embrace our truly unique and authentic selves. This will allow us to have even more compassion and love for our unique bodies, minds, and souls. It is time for us to learn to authentically love and trust ourselves so that we can then truly love and trust others. But how do we do that?

For starters, we need to begin to develop better communication skills, and we need to beginning with ourselves. We need to ask and answer some questions really honestly:

1. **Do I genuinely love myself?** If your answer is yes, great! Continue doing what you have been doing. If your answer is no, then ask yourself a new question: what changes do I need to make within myself so that I can become a person who I can truly love, respect, and appreciate?

2. **Do I genuinely believe that I am worthy of love and belonging?** If you have absolutely everything you need right now, and you feel totally worthy of love and belonging, great. If not, ask yourself: what do I need in order to live my life feeling deserving of worthiness, authenticity, connection, and joy? You might be surprised to learn that one of the core building blocks of a greater sense of worthiness, love, and belonging is having the courage to be imperfect and to fully embrace your vulnerability.

   (See the TED lecture by Brene Brown, The Power of Vulnerability, http://www.ted.com/talks/brene_brown_on_vulnerability.html)

3. **Where do I want to live?** If you hate where you are living, move. Life is too short to live in an environment you despise; it sucks the energy right out of you. Living where you love is energizing and that radiant energy will ensure that people will want to be around you. When we get uncomfortable and restless, it usually means we are ready to grow and expand.

4. **What are some new skills I want to learn that I have been putting off, telling myself I just don't have the time?** Painting? Pottery? Tennis? A marathon? Now is the time to make the time. Start today. Pick up the phone or get out your computer and pull up the studio on the Internet and sign up for that class. Find your racket or your running shoes in the back of your closet. Even if you take a baby step, it is one step closer than you were before.

5. **As you take new actions and working your way toward your new goals, ask yourself every moment, "Is this action getting me closer to or farther away from my goal?"** If your answer is farther away, then shift and redirect yourself back toward actions that will take you closer to your goal. Remember the old saying, "The journey of a thousand miles begins with one step."

6. **Who are the people I want around me who nurture my soul, who will support me in my new goals, and who make me feel empowered?** If you are surrounded by people who criticize or drain you all the time, change your situation or your friends. That's not to say it's best to forget our difficult relationships or experiences. Each difficult person or experience in our life—sometimes the hardest people or experiences for us to love—is an opportunity to develop compassion and kindness. For our own health and well-being, we need to bless them all, for they have taken us as far as they could on our journey of love together in this life. And then finally, at last, the most loving thing we can do is to let go of all our anger, disappointment, and frustration toward them so we can move on to more satisfying experiences and truly supportive relationships.

7. **What spiritual practice do I truly resonate with?** We need to create daily spiritual practices that are truly alive for us. A resonate spiritual practice can mean different things to different people. For some, finding a quiet space in their day to reflect, pray and connect with their higher spiritual selves holds tremendous meaning and peace. For others, their spiritual practice can be in movement, such as in a tai chi class or walking a labyrinth. My own spiritual practice has evolved over the years. I find that the more I focus on seeing the energy and beauty of God in all the little details in life around me, the more I am in constant connection and communion with God. However, each of us must follow our own hearts and minds in all

matters of the spirit and find a spiritual practice that we can resonate with. Let both your heart and mind guide you to whatever feels right for you and helps you connect most deeply with the God of your own understanding.

All of these questions are designed to take us closer to ourselves and help us to design the kind of life we can feel good about. Each time we take a new step and feel closer to ourselves and the kind of life we have dreamed of, we gain more and more confidence. We also gain courage to try new things and learn that we are far more powerful than we ever dreamed we could be.

It has been said that the definition of courage is to feel the fear and do it anyway. I think this holds true for love, too.

From Me
To You...

Try making a list of the things you love, which includes things you love about yourself, others, and life. Start small, and very quickly, you will see your list begin to change and grow.

Here are a few ideas from my own love list to help get you started:

I love to walk on the beach, to be on or near water.

I love surprises and unplanned adventures.

I love to travel, to see new places, and to experience the foods, sights, stories, music, traditions, and history of each of these new places, people, and cultures of the world.

I love to read inspiring books, see inspiring movies, or hear stories where the human spirit triumphs over all obstacles, including, but not limited to: evil, self-doubt or the seemingly impossible.

Sometimes just making a list like the one above can shift our mood into a higher level of energy and consciousness such as gratitude and love.

The Buddha said, "Change your thoughts and you change your world." When we change our thoughts and understanding to include more love, compassion, connection, trust, and vulnerability, then anything is possible in our lives.

The word *grace* brings to mind many ideas at once. There is the soft, classic grace of Audrey Hepburn. There is the regal grace of Grace Kelly, princess of Monaco. There is even the tough grace of Katherine Hepburn.

My dear friend and minister, Eric, said, "Grace is anything that arises, descends or appears that is effortless. In dance, we call a dancer graceful who appears to be dancing with no effort or struggle. Then there is the grace of an alcoholic who wakes up one morning and says, 'I'm done with alcohol,' and then enrolls in a rehab program. Grace is any time we turn a corner internally. It's like when we talk about how we're gonna forgive someone, and then there is the moment when we realize it is actually happening, or we have actually turned a corner inside and actually done it. That's grace."

There is the grace you may say before meals. The before-meal grace ritual my kids and I created at our home is in the graceful and heroic tradition of *The Three Musketeers*. Before eating, every person around our table holds out his or her fork until they meet together with a "clink!" sound. Then we all say together, "All for one and one for all!" Then the forks are lifted in the air and we begin to eat and move into conversation.

But when I think of *true* grace, what stands out most strongly in my mind is my Aunt Bobbe.

Barbara Pauley Pagen was a student at the University of California when she met Edwin Pauley, a regent of UCLA. They fell in love and got married, and "Bobbe" had many adventures over the course of her eighty-three years. She traveled the world. In fact, she was one of the first American women to go behind the Iron Curtain. She was a generous donor, and she and her husband built many things to help others: a wing of the Los Angeles Art Museum, and the sports facility on the UCLA campus called the Pauley Pavilion. She was very active in the restoration of her historic childhood home, the McHenry Mansion in Modesto, California. Her father was one of the original cattle ranchers there, and her family helped to settle the town. In fact, there is still a McHenry Boulevard in Modesto named after the McHenry family.

Bobbe was a consummate and graceful hostess. When John F. Kennedy came to visit their home, she sat him in a chair embroidered with the words, "The President's Chair." Bobbe hosted many heads of state, not only every president from Truman up through Carter, but also the king and queen of Jordan and the queen of Egypt. But all these achievements never went to Bobbe's head. She was always graceful and gracious no matter who was at the table.

One of my favorite stories about Bobbe is one that shows her true grace under pressure. I accompanied her to many a black-tie fundraiser. One night, she was in her gorgeous red, floor-length, low-cut gown with a huge red bow on the side. I noticed that she was coming my way with an unusual smile pasted on her face. As she held her smile, looking out over the crowd, Bobbe leaned over to me and whispered into my ear, "Mary Anne! My prosthesis from my mastectomy just fell out of my gown, and I kicked it under the table here. Can you get it and meet me in the bathroom in two minutes?" And then she was off, swirling her gown as she swept out of the room.

I sat down at the table and tried to think of the best way to handle this. I leaned over and saw that her very large prosthesis had gone under the table far into the center. I wondered how in the world I was going to get to it, let alone sneak it into the ladies' room! Then I had a sudden inspiration. I pretended to have a coughing fit, grabbed a napkin, and dove under the table. I managed to cover most of the prosthesis with the napkin, and I tucked it under my arm and crawled out from under the table on the far side closest to the door, hoping that no one would see me.

I did not have a large evening bag, so I just tucked the napkin-covered prosthesis under my arm and walked out. I found Bobbe in the ladies' room, and as soon as we saw each other, we started giggling hysterically. I held the prosthesis out to her and she snatched it, quickly stuffing it down her décolletage and repositioning both breasts so that they were even, saying, "Well! This is certainly proving to be a most interesting evening now, isn't it?"

I was still giggling and said, "Yes, Bobbe. It certainly is! This evening is definitely one for the history books!"

"I should say so. Well, Mary Anne, do I look even? In a couple of minutes I have to give a speech, and I don't want my breasts to suddenly start popping out all over the place during my talk."

"Yes, if you move your right breast a little more to the left you will look totally normal."

Bobbe quickly made one last adjustment and then raised her arm theatrically and said, "Well, Mary Anne, shall we? On with the show!" And with that, she whirled around and off we went back to the event. I was so proud watching the ever-so-graceful Bobbe at the podium giving her speech. Looking at her, you would never have known anything had ever happened.

*****

My aunt Bobbe lived a long life, full of adventures, and she was the most generous and grace-filled person I have ever known. I wish she were still alive to see the publication of this book, since we often talked about me publishing my own stories someday. This chapter is dedicated to her, in honor of the grace of her presence in my life.

Think about someone in your life who is still living who you would like to thank for the grace of their love and support. Why not send them a note today to tell them how much their grace and love has meant to you? It will mean the world to them.

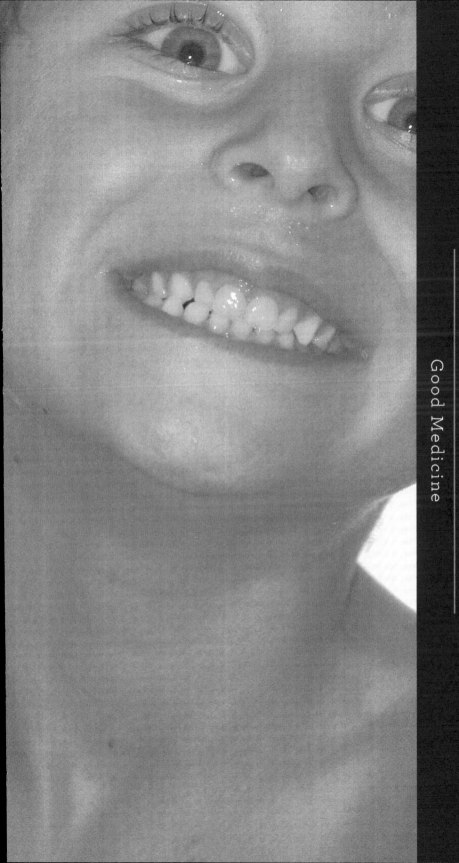

The actual term "humor" derives from the "humoral medicine" of the ancient Greeks. In Greek medicine, physicians were taught that the balance of fluids in the human body, known as humors, controlled human health and emotion. I believe that humor in our lives is as vital to us as our blood. I've also learned that mean, sarcastic, or cruel humor can drain the lifeblood out of you in a split second.

A wonderful Japanese proverb that speaks brilliantly to humor used as a weapon: "The tongue is but three inches long, yet it can kill a man six feet tall."

If you have a lot of heavy alcohol drinkers or drug users among your family or friends, you may have watched humor being used as a weapon or means of control. There's nothing funny about this kind of humor. Quite often, alcoholics and drug users feel free to say the meanest and most outrageous things, all under the guise of "Oh, c'mon. It was just a joke." They will justify their verbal barbs with comments like "Hey, I thought it was funny, and so did everybody else. If you had been drinking (or using) with us, I'm quite sure you would have been laughing, too." Or: "Get a grip. You are way too sensitive."

If you rise to the bait and tell them their comment hurt your feelings, they might choose to turn the tables on you with different verbal harpoons such as, "What's the matter with you? Dontcha have a sense of humor?" or "Give me a break. I was drinking. I don't remember," or "I have no idea what you are talking about. I never said that."

One of the hardest things about living with alcoholics, drug users, or emotional abusers is that these kinds of comments are all common, even daily refrains. For them, demeaning another person is fun and a kind of verbal sport. And because they were "under the influence" they can always choose to get out of any responsibility for their actions or comments by saying they "don't remember." But being outright cruel is never OK, and the sooner we remove ourselves from being around these kinds of people, the better for our own health and well-being.

*****

It was a relief to learn from my research on humor that there aren't any people or cultures around the world that do not have a sense of humor or any people who do not have the capacity to laugh or smile at something funny. But it is interesting that the extent to which an individual will find something humorous depends upon many variables: their geographical location, their culture, their level of maturity and intelligence, their level of education, and the context in which a particular joke was delivered.

One day, I posted an entry on my My Real Voice blog (www.myrealvoice.com/blog) entitled, "Public Speaking Jokes: Don't Let the Joke Be on You." One of my readers asked:

> "I read your blog on public speaking jokes. I'm a little confused. Are you saying humor in speeches is a bad thing? When is humor appropriate and what kind of jokes are okay?"

I think it is an excellent question and one that has been asked by more than one public speaker.

Self-effacing humor can be quite effective. Many executives that I know tell a little story about themselves or their families that illustrates their point. One well-known executive in Seattle is famous for his "Maddie stories." Every speech he gives includes a little anecdote that is the latest shared moment of connection with his daughter, Maddie. His "Maddie stories" have become a tradition for his loyal listeners, like an ongoing radio story. For a CEO with a regular audience, this approach can be quite endearing, allowing his listening employees a little glimpse into his private life, as well as an opportunity to learn more about what is truly important to him. It lets his audience to relate to him on a human level and this can go a long way toward creating rapport.

But humor doesn't always have to be in words. Some of my clients choose to put up a picture or a comic or a quote at the beginning of their presentation before they even make their PowerPoint presentation. That can be quite effective, too, and creates the expectation that this presentation is going to be really creative or interesting or thought provoking. As the speaker, you don't necessarily need to even comment on what's on the screen, if you don't want to.

One of my clients, a highly regarded cancer doctor at the Fred Hutchinson Cancer Research Center, came to me with a challenge she didn't know how to solve. She felt that she wanted to get some humor into her speech, and yet there didn't seem to be much funny material written or spoken about colon cancer. So we took a different approach.

Since this physician was well-known for her expert research in her field, I asked her to look in the comics for something related to advancements in medicine. In the comics, she found a drawing of a very old man standing at Saint Peter's gate, waiting in line to get into heaven. He finally gets to the front of the line and with this expression of bewilderment and hands raised high, the man exclaims to Saint Peter, "Hey, I would have been here much sooner without the advancements of modern medicine!"

With this comic alone, this well-regarded female physician set the entire tone at the beginning of her speech. We used this comic for another strategy, too. This funny but poignant statement in the comic also allowed my client to begin her speech with a perfect advance lead-in: it allowed her to talk about all the many advancements that had been made by her and her team at Fred Hutchinson Cancer Research Center, as well as to acknowledge others in the audience who were her respected colleagues in her field. This demonstrated her well-respected style of camaraderie, acknowledgment, and teamwork. The comic also let the audience know that this woman's speech wasn't going to be the usual long list of rather boring facts and numbers and graphs and charts that were normally expected at these high-level medical conferences.

This comic served another purpose as well. Like the majority of my clients, this highly regarded doctor was very nervous about giving a speech in front of her colleagues. Also, as most truly competent professionals do, she feared negative judgment, and an onslaught of criticism. The well-chosen comic, placed at the beginning of her speech, created a shared moment of laughter, which brought the audience to attention and together in a common bond of humor and shared experience.

The time the audience spent laughing gave this doctor, who walked slowly with a cane, some very valuable moments to get on stage, to adjust to being at the podium, to take a few deep breaths, and to take in her audience without feeling rushed, and also to smile herself. The comic also helped her to feel connected to her audience, and soothed the critical, judgmental voices in her head with a moment of shared connection with her audience through humor.

So while the use of humor in general is not a bad choice, the way that humor is delivered that makes all the difference.

From Me
To You...

This is the sweetest and dearest description that I know of laughter and the deep love it inspires in us. It's from *The Little Prince,* written by Antoine De Saint-Exupery:

"I have a present for you." The Little Prince laughed again.

"Ah little fellow, little fellow, I love hearing that laugh!"

"That'll be my present. Just that..."

"What do you mean?"

"People have stars, but they aren't the same....When you look up at the sky at night, since I'll be living on one of them, for you it'll be as if all the stars are laughing. You'll have stars that can laugh!"

And he laughed again....

"And it'll be as if I have given you, instead of stars, a lot of tiny bells that know how to laugh..."

And he laughed again.

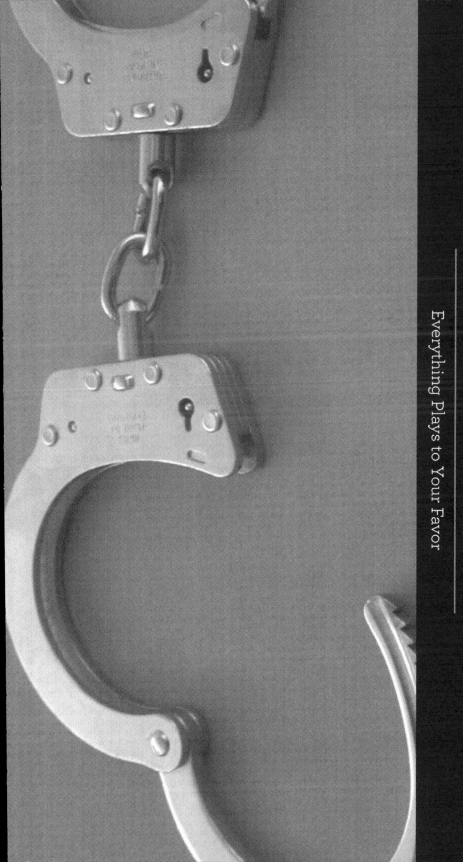

Possibility

Everything Plays to Your Favor

"All right, every day ain't going to be the best day of your life, don't worry about that. If you stick to it, you hold the possibility open that you will have better days."

—Wendell Berry

I think it is so interesting how many possibilities there are for the communication of messages directly to our souls, or our inner intuitive guidance that "speaks" to us about other ways we can consider any situation.

The morning after I broke up with a boyfriend who I really thought I was going to marry, I was feeling rather unsettled about it. However, I went to my e-mail inbox and found this "Note from the Universe" waiting for me:

> Whenever something doesn't work out the way you thought it would, Mary Anne, instead of thinking that something went wrong, see it as something that went unexpectedly well, but for reasons that are not yet apparent.
> Everything plays to your favor.
> Score!
>
> The Universe
> PS: And then keep on keeping on, Mary Anne.

(These Notes from the Universe are written five days a week by Mike Dooley, and you can sign up for them at www.tut.com)

That evening, in my meditation class, we were going over the final chapter of Raymond Holliwell's wonderful book, Working with the Law. One of the sections that jumped off the page of the book for me was:

> Whatever your present state or condition may be, there is a better and larger future in store for you, but you must prepare yourself for it. You cannot rise into the better and greater things unless you DO SOMETHING about it...It is the Law's intention that you shall move forward...In the end you will be compelled to move forward, especially in the direction of the soul's growth.

When I was driving home after my class, I noticed this on a church marquee: What looks like an ending may be a wonderful new beginning.

What did these three messages all have in common? Possibilities. And what do all possibilities have in common? More possibilities!

But sometimes, I have to admit, the positive possibilities can be really hard to see. It really helps to get the perspective of a trusted professional therapist or friend. After breaking up with my boyfriend, who I really thought was "*the one*," I marched myself right back into therapy. I really needed perspective on the fact that when my boyfriend finally revealed his true colors, I discovered that both he and his son were abusive alcoholics.

When I sat down, I blurted out to my therapist, Robin, "How could this happen to me of all people? I have had so much therapy, I have read all the books, I grew up with alcoholics, you would think, by now, I would recognize the signs! How in the world could I have not seen it?"

Robin looked at me with her kind eyes, in her "mother bear" body with her cockeyed smile, and said simply, "He felt like home."

"What? 'He felt like home?' What does that mean?"

"I think you believe on some level, even though we both know it is not true, that you are not lovable. So, as a result of that belief you have about yourself, you keep letting people into your life who reinforce that feeling."

I was confused. My head was spinning. "What feeling, Robin? Are you saying that I'm not lovable?"

"Let me put it a different way. For better or worse, when a person has lived in an abusive home growing up, they tend to gravitate to that same experience over and over in their later relationships with lovers, bosses, and friends because it feels really familiar. So, that's what I mean when I say, 'He felt like home.'"

This really struck a chord with me deep down. "Am I pathetic or what?" I said, as tears began to stream down my face.

"No, you are not pathetic. But you did want it to work," Robin said simply.

"Wanted *what* to work?!" I cried.

"You wanted the relationship with this man to work," Robin said again.

"Yes, you're right, I did. Robin, I really did. I introduced him to all my close friends. We did fun things together. I loved him. And I have to admit, he had some really great qualities. But he and his son both had very serious drinking problems. Jeez, I very nearly married the guy! I think that's what scares me more than anything else." I cried, holding my head in my hands.

"You really, really wanted it to work," Robin said.

Robin let the silence lay there for a bit, and then she asked, "Tell me, when was the moment that finally made you absolutely sure you did not want to marry this man? In other words, when was it you knew you were not going to *stay* with this man?"

"It was the night my daughter and I had gone over to his home for dinner. Suddenly, in a blinding flash of the obvious, I realized that I had ignored all the signs. When it came right down to it, he was an alcoholic and I had refused to see it. He showed me that night that he was scary and an abusive bully, and suddenly, my entire future with this man simply evaporated right before my eyes. Then Sarah and I left his house.

"In the car, I told Sarah, 'I am leaving this relationship. I am *done*. No one will *ever* abuse someone I love. *Never*.'

"Sarah was puzzled. 'What? You are leaving him? I thought you loved him and wanted to marry him?'

"'I did, but I don't anymore. No one has a right to be abusive to you or to me. I don't care who they are. I am *done*.'

"'Are you sure, Mom? Are you sure you want to do that? I mean, I know you said he had many fine qualities. Maybe this was just an isolated thing.'

"'No, Sarah, there is way too much alcohol being consumed, and now I have seen both him and his son become abusive. That's it.'

"'That's it? Just like that?' Sarah said, shaking her head in what looked like a mixture of confusion and wonder.

"'Just like that,' I said, nodding. 'I just wish I had been able to do enough to stop it and protect you from seeing it.'

"'Actually, you did, Mom,' Sarah said, gently. 'We're driving away right now, safe and sound, aren't we?' Sarah put a hand on my shoulder and gave me a pat. 'Thank you, Mom.' And then we both burst into tears as we drove to the ferry dock."

Robin sighed loudly as I finished the story. "Wow. You really, really wanted that relationship with him to work out. And it didn't. I am so genuinely sorry. But I am also happy that you were able to protect your daughter. You did really great."

I smiled. That was why I had come: to get her mama-bear reassurance that I had done well, despite how scary it had been for me.

"And you may not realize it now, but you also did it for all the future women in your family who come after her, too."

"Funny thing, Robin," I said, smiling and shaking my head. "I am actually grateful he came into my life. After we left, I was able to say to him in e-mails what I had always wanted to say to all those other people in my life who had become abusive when they were drinking. And now that it's over, I feel both grateful and incredibly relieved. But, how do I make absolutely sure I don't let this ever happen again?"

"Well, here's what I think about that," Robin said. "First, you ask a lot of good questions. Then you pay close attention to how much he drinks. You observe and you learn. Most importantly, you pay special attention to when the hairs on the back of your neck go up. That signals danger. And if someone *ever* becomes in *any* way disrespectful towards you, you *leave*, right then. No need to apologize or explain yourself. *You just leave.* And you don't look back."

"Robin, I think the most important exchange we had was when he said, 'Wow, you must really love me to stay with me through all this.' I said, 'Actually, through the time I have spent with you, I've made an important decision for myself. I no longer choose to be around a man who has a problem with alcohol, who is emotionally unpredictable, or with whom I don't feel safe. And therefore I no longer choose to be in a relationship with you.'" Robin gave me a *high five* on that. This man proved to be a wonderful opportunity for me to finally seize the possibility of a different, unlimited future. As a result, I am now ready to meet a new man who will be the true Mr. Wonderful of my dreams. What possibilities!

As Holliwell says, "Obstacles seen from a higher view are stepping-stones instead."

From Me
To You...

Here is another wonderful and encouraging concept from Holliwell's book:

"Scientific research into the mysteries of the human mind reveals a wonderful world of power and possibility. The psychological truth is that what is possible to one mind is possible to another, and vastly more than we ever dreamed."

So imagine a world in which you saw not barriers, but infinite possibilities everywhere you looked. Wherever you see a perceived limitation, investigate. Is it, in fact, a limitation, or an open invitation toward a new possibility? Possibilities are everywhere if we choose to see them.

Hope

A Drop in the Bucket

I had the privilege of coaching the first woman to ever run for Parliament in Mongolia. Her name was Battsetseg, or "Baagi" for short. At the time I met Baagi, she was the vice president of the Democratic Women's Union in Mongolia. She and eight of her female colleagues—doctors, lawyers, and media professionals—each saved the equivalent of a year's salary to come to the United States, such was their drive to achieve their goal: democracy for the people of Mongolia.

When we began our conversation in my campaign school, I had no idea what it was like in Mongolia, if we would have anything in common, or if the language barrier would be too great a divide. I soon found that we had more in common than we would have ever dreamed.

In my role as an American political consultant, I had so many questions in my mind about the Mongolian culture, how voting was conducted, the age ranges of the voters, location and primary concerns of the different voting blocks, what each age range cared about in terms of the issues, how voting is usually conducted, and many other areas of concern that need to be clarified when building a solid campaign.

But when I met these amazing women, the first thing I said was, "Honestly, I don't have the slightest idea about what it is like to be a Mongolian person. Please help me get inside the head of a Mongolian woman and man. Are they different or similar?" This question lit a fire of excitement in the women.

The discussion was lively. I wrote out the answers to each question on large sheets of paper, and when we hung them up to see the big picture, they covered the entire room.

Toward the end of our discussion, I asked: "How do you think the average Mongolian person votes? With fear, anger, hope, or trust?" This question stopped them, and everyone went silent for a moment. And then the room erupted in cross-dialogue as the women debated this issue. The translator was trying to keep up with the conversation, but everyone was talking so fast she finally gave up and looked at me and shrugged her shoulders.

The spirited debate lasted for more than fifteen minutes. Finally, consensus appeared to have been reached. The translator finally stood up and said, "We have decided that the average Mongolian person votes with hope."

"Wow, that is so interesting," I said. "Because when we vote in this country, we seem to vote with anger as we say, 'Get that jerk outta there!' Or we vote with fear when we ask ourselves, 'Who is the lesser of two evils?'" All of the women nodded appreciatively.

I continued, "But here is the most interesting thing: I was coming up in the elevator on my way here and a man got into the elevator with me. He noticed that I had all this work stuff under my arms and said, 'Oh, giving a lecture today?' I said, 'Well, no. I am actually a political consultant, and I'm coming here to meet with the first women ever to run for Parliament in Mongolia.'

"He suddenly got a very stern and condescending look on his face. He said. 'Oh, you gonna teach 'em how to cheat and lie, now are ya?'"

"I was honestly shocked at his comment and replied, 'No. Actually, I am going to try to give them some hope!'

"At this, the man gave a little sound like 'Harrumph!' as if to say, 'Yeah, sure you are!' and walked out at the next floor.

"I have been thinking of his comment ever since, and I am so glad to hear from you all here today that the Mongolian people vote with hope. So let's talk about that hope. What does hope mean to each one of you here, individually?"

The women all thought for a few moments, silently. Then they erupted, full of passion. Through the translator, they said things like, "I think it is about the possibility of a better future." Another said, "Yes. It is a future we can get behind and believe in." "It is full of possibilities." "It feels warm." "It feels like I can contribute something valuable to make the future better." "A better world for our children."

They were talking with their hands in front of them now, as they described a world full of hope. It was the most animated discussion of the entire day. I felt this was a good place to finish our day of training, on an up note, and we all left feeling hopeful about Mongolia's future.

But this story of hope does not end there. We kept in touch by e-mail, and from the other side of the world—Seattle— I guided them all the way through in their campaigns. Unlike the United States, where the presidential campaign process can start years before the actual election day, in Mongolia they have exactly forty-five days of campaigning before the date of the election.

It was a very exciting race. Baagi went from fourth place to third, then to second, and was closing in on first place in the polls, when the Communists began accelerating their purchase of the vote. In Eastern Bloc countries, politics is a blood sport. This election was no different. People were being given money to vote for the Communist candidate. When the day of the vote finally came, the Communist Party candidate was "elected."

That's when the riots broke out.

Some 6,000 kids between the ages of eighteen and twenty-two began rioting, protesting about how the election was "fixed." Here's what happened, in Baagi's own words:

> This election was one of the worst elections in my life. Our party lost and Revolutionary party...showed us the worst election in Mongolia. They learned it from Russia. They almost didn't do campaign and meetings. They just sheeted and gave money to the voters. After the election First of July, there was demonstration within 6,000 young people and some of them killed and 700 are in the jail. They beat them and there is no human rights protection. We lost our control. All things they do is very much Communist way.
>
> I hate this and cannot stay at home and cannot sleep.
>
> What we need to do? Where is the philosophy of a Democratic world that we started 18 years ago? I cannot see this and don't want to be citizen of this country. Every thing miss. 700 young people are in the jail and we cannot go on the street now.
>
> Please keep in touch and pray for us.
>
> Love you,
>
> Baagi

Democracy is a hard movement to birth anywhere, anytime in the world. As with any struggle, great or small, there are many elements that come into play when achieving success. Encouragement, hard work, and hey, let's face it, luck, are all major factors. But the bottom line is always hope. They say, "Hope springs eternal," and I think that's true. The spring that we draw from is inside ourselves. After becoming very depressed at the outcome of her election, Baagi found her courage and went on to run again. Baagi has become a great woman leader for democracy in her country, Mongolia.

So in the face of any great disappointment, disaster, pain, or illness, we always have the choice to have hope, wherever we are in the world. If we human beings have even one shred of hope, even a whiff, we always have the capacity to hold on to that hope and keep going through anything that we may face in our lives.

From Me
To You...

It is said by the masters that even a little poison can cause death, and even a tiny seed can become a huge tree. The Buddha said: "Do not overlook negative actions merely because they are small; however small a spark may be, it can burn down a haystack as big as a mountain."

Similarly he said: "Do not overlook tiny good actions, thinking they are of no benefit; even tiny drops of water in the end will fill a huge vessel."

Perspective

From Solomon to Woody

One perspective that I have deeply relied on in more than one occasion to get me through tough times on more than one occasion is: "This too shall pass." Once there was a powerful king who asked his wise men to create a ring that would make him happy when he was sad, and vice versa. After much deliberation, the sages handed him a simple ring with the words "This too will pass," etched on it.

Other Peoples' Perspectives

There is a story about a Buddhist monk in a small town, who lived alone in his house on the edge of town. People would come to him, and knock on his gate, and bring offerings of rice and other food, saying, "Ah, Master, you are such a good example for us all. We are grateful you live in our town."

And the Master would bow and say calmly, "So you say."

After a few years, a young woman who was doing house cleaning for the monk accused him of raping her and of being the father of her baby. At this point, the townspeople came to the monk's gate and threw rocks and said, "You are a wicked, bad monk, taking advantage of a young woman like that!"

And the Master bowed and said calmly, "So you say."

The townspeople shunned him and stopped bringing gifts. But the monk took the young woman in and raised her son for many years. Finally, when the son went off to school, the woman confessed to the town that she had had a one-night stand twenty years before with a man passing through town and that the monk was not the father. The townspeople felt terrible and they all ran to his gate and said, "Oh, dear monk. We misjudged you. You are indeed an honorable man and did right by this woman. We are so sorry. Please accept our gifts. You are a fine monk, and we are blessed to have you live among us."

And the Master bowed once again and said calmly, "So you say."

A Humorous Perspective

"Comedy is tragedy, plus time."

"If it bends, it's comedy. If it breaks, it isn't."

(Thanks, Woody Allen, for those words of wisdom.)

From Me
To You...

People can call us names or say whatever they want about us. Life will provide us countless opportunities to model dignity and restraint. Ultimately, it is we who need to dig deep within ourselves, hold our heads up, stay true to our perspective of who we know we are, believe in that truth of who we are, and move on. We don't ever have to allow ourselves to get attached to what another person says to us. Just because they say it, doesn't make it true. No matter what, our answer can always be, "So you say."

Truth

The Burden of Proof

Much of my life, I have defined myself by what others said I could not do. One year, when I was doing my first season of summer-stock theater, we had a Sunday off and we were taken to a nearby lake for a day of rest and relaxation. It was a beautiful, sunny day, and the temperature was in the midseventies. A group of us decided to go waterskiing.

After we all piled into the boat, one of the guys pointed to a large ski ramp out in the middle of the lake. "No woman could ever do that," he said, offhandedly.

I said, "'Scuse me? What did you say?"

"I *said*," he replied sarcastically, "No *woman* could *ever* do *that*."

"Oh yeah?" I said. "Just watch me! Let's take the boat over there." I was hooked. On behalf of myself and all other women in the world, I was compelled to prove this man wrong and show him that women could, indeed, do anything they set their minds to. These are the times when I know my Guardian Angel calls in for reinforcements and shudders in her wings.

This kind of thing had happened to me many times before. Over the years, if people said things like "No woman can do that," or "It's not possible," or "You can't do that," I just didn't seem to be able to stop myself. I rose to the bait. In hindsight, I realize that this day, I was prepared to lay my life on the line to prove something to some guy. It wasn't the first time I had done that, and it certainly was not the last.

I put on the pair of shoddy skis in the boat. While I had waterskied since childhood, I never had gone up over a ski jump before. But I figured, *How hard can this be?* The closer I got to the huge wooden jump in the middle of the lake, I began to see just how huge and formidable it was. In fact, it became terrifying the closer the boat took me towards it. But I was a woman on a mission, and I wasn't about to let go of the rope.

Without any experience or instruction, I guessed that I needed to line myself off to the right to take the jump and allow the boat to pass by on the left of the jump. I hit the very steep ramp with a slam and it was a very weird sensation going from 31 mph on water to slamming into solid wood. BAM! is what you hear but then your skis also SLAM! to a stop, and you start slowly grinding up at about a forty-five-degree angle toward the top of the jump. Yikes!

But I couldn't let go of the rope or I would tumble backwards over this very splintery platform. On the other hand, the closer I got to the top and saw how high I was, I couldn't let go of the rope because I could crack my head open on the top of the jump.

About halfway up the ramp, I thought to myself, *What the heck am I doing?* But I had to keep my concentration, so I wouldn't kill myself. There was no turning back, and I had to concentrate hard as I reached the top of the very steep ramp. I had no idea what was coming next.

As the tips of my skis cleared the top of the ramp I could see the boat far away in the water. I was still holding on to the ski rope handle as the backs of the skis cleared the top of the jump. But as soon as I went off the jump and flew up suspended high in the air, I freaked.

I was holding on tight to a ski rope with my skis dangling every which way! And I was speeding up! As you start coming down off of a ski jump, you speed up as you get closer to the water and come into line with the boat.

But I did not know any of that, and as I freaked, I let go of the ski rope and began to fall like a stone down toward the lake. In free fall, I had just about enough time to think to myself, *This is not good.* I slammed into the lake on the top of my mismatched skis, and it hurt. A lot.

When the boat came around to pick me up, and I saw that guy laughing as if to say, "Told ya so!" I couldn't help myself. Rather than say, "Pick me up. I'm hurt. My left knee feels like it is on fire," I said instead, "Take me up again!" and I swam to my skis, picked them up, put them on, and grabbed the rope.

What Was I Thinking?

The first time up, I had no idea what to expect from a ski jump, and my rational brain had temporarily been on vacation somewhere. But, the second time—well, it was nothing short of terrifying. Still, I had something to prove. I was going to make that jump, no matter what it took.

I never thought to ask myself, *So, again, why is it you care what that idiot guy thinks? And why is it that you feel compelled to do this on behalf of "women everywhere?"* Instead what was going through my head was, *I'll show* him. *Yeah. No matter what it takes, I'll show him.* Whenever I think about this skiing day, I actually shudder to think of how close I came to killing myself for absolutely no other reason than pride.

Over the Jump a Second Time

So there we were, the boat lining up to the side of the ramp with me coming into line behind and then cutting sharply over to the right to hit the ramp, both ski tips up. Only this time, my left knee was burning so much, I could barely hold myself standing up. But it was too late to turn back. I was grinding up at the forty-five-degree angle toward the top.

All I kept saying to myself was, *"You can* do *this. You can* do *this. YOU CAN DO THIS!"* And that's about all the time I had before I was airborne. This time as I was flying up in the air, I was absolutely *determined* to hold on to the rope. As I gritted my teeth and held on for dear life, I began to descend slowly and steadily and then picked up speed the closer I got to the water. I held on and held on and held on, all the while repeating in my head, *You can* do *this. You can* do *this. YOU CAN DO THIS!*

Suddenly I hit the water hard, both skis in line, there was a fraction of a second where everything was still, and then the boat jerked me forward with a sudden slam, giving me what instantly felt like whiplash in my neck, not to mention the feeling of both my arms being pulled out of their sockets. My knees hurt like crazy from the previous jump, too, but still I held on to that ski rope.

I held on just long enough to catch the eyes of the jerk in the boat and give him a look like, *Oh yeah, no woman can do this? Well this woman just did, you jerk!* And as soon as I caught his eye and delivered my message with my eyes and absolutely no words, I let go of the rope.

I got back into the boat and grabbed a towel since my teeth were chattering. I must have been slowly going into shock because when we got back to the dock and I stepped out of the boat, my left leg collapsed. I not only could not walk, I couldn't stand.

I had to think fast at that moment because my employers had observed my little "stunt" from the beach and were coming our way. When a few other actors rushed over, I said in a whisper, "Help me off the dock. My knee is not working. Don't tell anybody. Pretend I am fine to the boss and let's just start laughing. Hurry, go!"

And inside I was thinking, *Oh God, I'm in some serious trouble here. This was a very bad idea. God, what was I thinking?* God and I have had this same chat numerous times over the course of my life.

My actor buddies covered me; we all smiled, and I cheerfully waved to my boss as my friends poured me into a car to go back to the theater. We spent the next several hours trying to figure out how I was going to explain to the boss why I needed to go onstage on crutches that night in *Fiddler on the Roof.*

Once my adrenaline had worn off, I knew I had done a very dangerous thing. Not only had I risked my neck and been seriously injured, I had risked my job: I was twenty-one years old and had twenty-four dollars left in my checking account. This summer-stock job was all I had, and I had jeopardized it just to prove to some jerk that he was wrong and I was right.

The Burden of Truth

I have asked myself many times why I took that risky chance with my life. A pattern in my behavior that day on the lake that was merely indicative of a larger pattern at work within my life that I really needed to understand before I inadvertently got myself killed.

The truth of this pattern became very clear one day while speaking with my therapist, Dr. S. After relaying this and several similarly terrifying episodes, Dr. S. said, "You know, Mary Anne? It seems to me that you have spent your entire life defining yourself by what other people have said you could not do. Do you want to continue to live like that? Defined by other people and what they say you cannot do?"

I had to think hard about that. Finally I said, "You know? I think you are right. I have always tried to prove everybody wrong, especially when a man says I can't do something. It's like I can't help myself. I get in some sort of tractor beam. It's so weird."

Dr. S. sat in his chair with his pen poised over his pad and said, "The real question here is, do you know the truth of why you keep doing this over and over to yourself?"

"Nope."

"Hmm. Seems to me that you are trying to really prove you are smart enough, strong enough, capable enough to someone. Is it you? If it's not you, who is it? Are you letting the entire rest of the world define you for you?"

"Uh, yeah." I frowned, trying to get a breath of air. "I think I have lived my entire life like that. Defined by other people. And what they said I could not do."

"Do you honestly think that's an effective strategy? By that I mean, has it made you happy? Has it made you feel good about yourself?" Dr. S. asked, quietly.

"Uh, I would have to say no, Dr. S. All it's done is cause me a whole lot of pain and suffering. For the majority of my life."

Dr. S. just nodded.

I had a sudden stomach ache. "Ouch. This truth really hurts."

"Before you go, Mary Anne, I would just like to say a couple of things. I think you are too trusting. People who are too trusting tend to trust others' opinions and reflections more than their own truth and the truth of their own experiences."

"Oh, so I should trust myself more? Is that what you are suggesting?"

"Well, I think you will live a heck of a lot longer if you do. And actually, I think the truth of who you really are is quite exceptional. But please, don't take my word for it," Dr. S. said with a sly grin.

So what do I truly believe is "the truth" about me? Well, I have discovered that there are many truths and that the ones I most value in both myself and others are kindness, compassion and empathy.

I also understand that I have a different responsibility to myself. Now when I hear someone say, "A woman can't do *x*," I don't get hooked like I so automatically and reflexively used to. I ask myself, *Is that really true?* and *"What do I think? What do I believe?* and *Is this my battle to fight at this moment in time?* and *What else could this be about for me?* I ask all these questions before leaping in without thinking things through, most of the time running my decisions through the truth of my own gut. I certainly am clear on one point for sure: I don't need to defend all of womanhood against every loser who comes along. I now know from experience that I can trust my instincts and that it's not my job to prove anything to anybody.

From Me
To You...

So what is the real truth of who you are? Is what you currently believe about yourself the actual "truth," or are you living up to some ideal or expectation of someone else in your life from your past, such as a spouse or parent or teacher? If you now recognize any current "truth" about yourself that isn't really yours, what would you change?

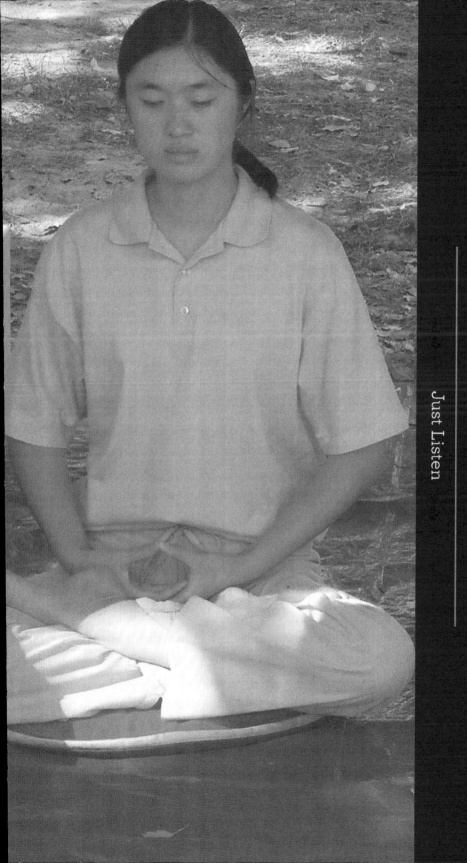

Intuition

Just Listen

"The only real valuable thing is intuition," said Albert Einstein, one of the most brilliant minds of our century. I would have to agree that my intuition has guided me all through of my life, even if at times I was not exactly sure what it was saying.

Most of the time when my intuition was clearest, I would have an "Oh no, I have a really, really, really bad feeling about this," kind of intuition. That doesn't mean I always followed it though. Sometimes my head would instruct, "Go right," and my heart would give me the intuition of, "Go left." I can say that most times when I trusted my heart over my head, things usually turned out better for me. I am convinced that the heart is the bigger brain.

I've spoken to many different people about their experiences of intuition, and have found that in practically all professions and walks of life, for most people, their intuition was both grounding and freeing. It didn't seem to matter whether they were talking about faith or math or music or acting or politics.

Most of those people agreed that intuition is extremely important to them, and they try to follow their intuition as best they can. Even more interesting is that at the same time, each person I spoke with also had their own unique definition of intuition that made sense to them, and there are even more examples throughout literature.

The following are some of my favorite perspectives on intuition:

"Faith is a passionate intuition."
  —William Wordsworth

"Cease trying to work everything out with your minds. It will get you nowhere. Live by intuition and inspiration and let your whole life be revelation."
  —Eileen Caddy

"But, you know, when I choose a film, I need to believe in it and believe I can do something special with it, and after a while that means not trying to judge or analyze why I should do it. You have to follow this intuition thing, which is a mystery to me."
  —actress Juliette Binoche

But learning to trust our intuition is a way to connect us with our Higher Selves. For many of us, this may seem impossible because our thoughts and minds so often get in the way, making it hard for us to even hear what our intuition is telling us. But intuition usually wins out in the end, even if it takes years.

"Conversion for me was not a Damascus Road experience. I slowly moved into an intellectual acceptance of what my intuition had always known."
　　—Madeleine L'Engle

"I feel there are two people inside me—me and my intuition. If I go against her, she'll screw me every time, and if I follow her, we get along quite nicely."
　　—actress Kim Basinger

"I never took sheet music seriously. I could do better myself just by listening to other people and using my own intuition."
　　—musician Brian May

"I somehow sensed when I was a teenager that I wanted to do my own work. I was quite clear that I didn't want to be an interpretative kind of artist. I had an intuition about wanting to create my own form, in one way or another, whatever that would be."
　　—artist Meredith Monk

"Nobody taught Picasso how to paint—he learned for himself. And nobody can teach you to be a producer. You can learn the mechanics, but you can't learn what's right about a script or a director or an actor. That comes from instinct and intuition. It comes from inside you."
　　—producer Dino De Laurentiis

"Thus, in a sense, mathematics has been most advanced by those who distinguished themselves by intuition rather than by rigorous proofs."
　　—mathematician Felix Klein

"Intuition is a spiritual faculty and does not explain, but simply points the way."
　　—Florence Scovel Shinn

So what is the speed of intuition?

"Intuition is reason in a hurry."
  — Holbrook Jackson

"Intuition is the clear conception of the whole at once."
  —Johann Kaspar Lavater

How can we use our intuition best?

"Intuition will tell the thinking mind where to look next."
  — Jonas Salk

"It is always with excitement that I wake up in the morning wondering what my intuition will toss up to me, like gifts from the sea. I work with it and rely on it. It's my partner."
  —Jonas Salk

Why should we listen to our intuition?

"Trusting our intuition often saves us from disaster."
  —Anne Wilson Schaef

"My gut and intuition told me it wasn't time to do this."
  —Mario Vazquez

"The creative is the place where no one else has ever been. You have to leave the city of your comfort and go into the wilderness of your intuition. What you'll discover will be wonderful. What you'll discover is yourself."
  —Alan Alda

"There is no logical way to the discovery of these elemental laws. There is only the way of intuition, which is helped by a feeling for the order lying behind the appearance."
  —Albert Einstein

"No matter how deep a study you make, what you really have to rely on is your own intuition and when it comes down to it, you really don't know what's going to happen until you do it."
  —Konosuke Matsushita

"Roosevelt's humor was broad, his manner friendly. Of wit there was little; of philosophy, none. What did he possess? Intuition, inspiration, love of adventure."
—Emanuel Celler

But by accessing our innermost self, we will find that the information we receive is usually what we truly need at that moment. The more we allow our bodies to open up and share with us the connection it has with our deeper self, the better we can truly access the knowledge we hold so deeply within. Our beings are capable of extremely deep insights, and our intuition will always help us find the answers we seek.

"The smallest flower is a thought, a life answering to some feature of the Great Whole, of whom they have a persistent intuition."
—Honore De Balzac

From Me
To You...

Supermodel **Gisele Bundchen** reminds us:

"The more you trust your intuition, the more empowered you become, the stronger you become, and the happier you become."

Today, find a quiet place, sit down, close your eyes, and ask your own intuition how you could become more empowered, stronger, and happier.

And then just listen.

Wish

It's More Than Rubbing a Lamp

Many people make a wish before they blow the candles out on their birthday cake. Others imagine what three wishes they would make if a Genie suddenly appeared out of a magic lantern and said in a big booming voice, "Your wish is my command!" In our family, wishing is a cherished tradition.

When we spot a white horse out in the middle of a field, we all make a wish. If we are out on the freeway and a truck drives by with bales of hay piled high on the flat bed, we all break out into a chorus of: "Bales of hay! Bales of hay! Take my wish and ride away!" As I reflect back now, these "additional wish options" were originally suggested by my mother who was always trying to come up with new ways to keep my four brothers and me busy on long car trips!

Also thanks to my mother, I have always "sealed" every single wish I have ever made in the super, secret, special way she taught me. It's so fun, I want to share it with you!

Official Instructions for Sealing Your Wish

Step One: Open your left hand, palm facing up. Your left open palm is the "magic envelope" for your wish.

Step Two: Lick the tip of your right index finger. The tip of your right finger is the "glue" that will close your "magic wish envelope."

Step Three: Tap the tip of your right index finger into the middle of your left palm. Your "magic wish envelope" is now officially closed.

Step Four: Make a fist with your right hand and "stamp" your open left palm. Voila! This is the last and most important step to officially "send"your wish out into The Universe to the special place where all wishes go to be granted.

Even though I am a grown woman now, I still wish on the first star I see appear in the sky every night. I repeat this little rhyme: "Star light, star bright, first star I see tonight. Wish I may. Wish I might. Grant the wish I wish tonight!" In fact, I've never made a single wish in my life without "sealing it" just exactly the way my mother taught me. My kids seal their wishes exactly the same way. Now you can too!

Here is another perspective on wishing from author Richard Bach: "You are never given a wish without also being given the power to make it come true.

You may have to work for them however." I like Bach's idea that our wishes arrive in our hearts and minds with all the power and creativity we need to make them come true. He suggests our wishes are inklings or hints about possibilities for our future and that they are born out of our innate abilities and talents. So perhaps our wishes are not out of our reach after all. We just need to be open to their possibilities and then supply the necessary "elbow grease" to make them come true.

Check this out: www.flyingwishpaper.com

A Whimsical Kit to Make Your Wishes Come True:

"Think of a special wish... your fondest dream, your deepest desire, your ambitions, concerns, or burdens—and write it down on the Flying Wish Paper®. Shape your paper into a tube and place it on the Wish Platform®. Light the top edge of the tube and watch it burn down in a small, beautiful flame. At the last moment, your wish magically lifts off the platform and rises to the heavens!"

The true connections of our lives are often made in the strangest ways, in the most improbable circumstances and with the most exquisite people. On the one hand, deep connections can be built with people over a lifetime. But deep connections can also happen in an instant and with someone who, just a moment before, was a perfect stranger.

In Lisbon, Portugal, after I had visited the castle, I had a feeling, or what you might call a strong, intuitive impulse, that I should walk down a particular hill. At the time, I didn't really know why I was being pulled in that direction. However, I did know that this "pull" felt a lot like what had happened to me in a cathedral over twenty years before, after my son had died. So instead of turning left with everyone else, I turned to the right and started walking.

This pull got stronger and stronger as I reached the bottom of the hill, where a very large cathedral stood. I looked up and I noticed that it had a banner across the entrance that read in Portuguese, "Visita Das Reliquias de Santa Teresinha Do Menino Jesus. A Portugal. 28 Outubro a 15 Dezembro." Women were everywhere outside, heading into the cathedral. I joined them.

Once I entered the church, I could see that on the altar, there was a huge golden reliquary in the shape of a Gothic cathedral, encased in what looked like plastic or glass. There were women everywhere: quietly praying, sitting in the pews, or waiting in a line that went from the entrance to the reliquary. I joined them, curious as to what they were all waiting for. While I was in line, I noticed that there were huge banners of a young woman's face, with the words "Santa Teresinha" on each one.

I looked back at the altar. As each woman filed past the reliquary, she placed her keys, or a photograph, or a flower, or her fingertips on the reliquary's plastic case. Some stopped, bowed their heads, and then walked quietly by. Some knelt. Some cried. Each appeared to be asking for a blessing of some kind as they passed by the golden reliquary, which held a few bones of this long-dead saint. I watched and waited in line with everyone else for my turn.

Saint Thérèse of Lisieux was born Thérèse Martin in Alençon, France, in 1873. She entered the Lisieux Carmel convent at the age of fifteen. She spent her years in the convent in quiet contemplation. Studying and writing, Thérèse developed a simple faith based on the spirituality of childhood—a bold and confident trust in God. The spirituality of her "little way" was not about extraordinary things, but rather doing the simple things of life well and with extraordinary love.

Thérèse died of tuberculosis at the age of twenty-four. Most saints in the Catholic Church have achieved some measure of renown for having committed a "great act," a certifiable and unexplainable miracle. But it was Saint Thérèse's all-consuming faith, her simple love of and belief in God and all things holy that makes her special to many Catholics. For her simple faith and strong will alone, Saint Thérèse made the fast track to sainthood. Saint Thérèse was a woman after my own heart.

After I passed by the relics and asked for protection and a blessing for my children and myself, I went over and sat down to the left of the reliquary. From there, I could observe the other women as they went by. Near me was another woman people-watching, and I smiled at her.

She spoke only Portuguese and I only Spanish, but we tried to connect using the words we did have, and using our eyes and hand gestures to further communicate a point. We laughed as we pantomimed the fact that, as we each listened to the other, we understood about every fifth word. The rest we communicated with hands flying to our hearts and pointing to the women at the reliquary and smiling deep smiles. This lady and I agreed that we'd found the most perfect spot up close for observing everything.

She and I had both been sitting by the relics on the side for quite some time, and the cathedral was slowly filling up with even more people waiting to see the reliquary. They continued to very respectfully file by, one by one, kneeling in front of and touching the relics with their fingertips or anything they wanted a blessing on. Then, after touching the reliquary, each person would sit down to pray. Soon the cathedral was jammed on all sides with people.

It seemed that some sort of special Sunday service was to be held in honor of Saint Thérèse. My new friend and I felt very happy and smug, having come so early and having secured such a choice spot in the cathedral. And then, one of the priests came over to us and told us we would have to move. "Why?" we asked simultaneously in both Spanish and Portuguese. He explained to her, and then she to me, that the spot we were sitting in was the one spot in the cathedral reserved for the choir only.

She and I looked at each other with dismay and then at the crowds and then back at each other, and at the same time, we laughed and sighed and threw both our hands up in the air as if to say, "Oh well! So what can you do?" We stayed together and found another spot fairly close to stand and wait for the service to begin.

Some other ladies showed us a white scarf they had bought in the church store. It had the image of Saint Thérèse on it, along with the commemorative dates of her visit to Lisbon, Portugal. Although we wanted one of the scarves, neither my friend nor I wanted to take the chance of losing yet another good spot near the relics and the altar. Finally, she made a decision and pantomimed to me that she was going to try to get a scarf. She soon disappeared into the crowd, and I felt sad that she had gone.

All of a sudden there she was, returning to "our spot" with two scarves, one for me and one for her. She said that she had heard the voice of Saint Thérèse in her ear, telling her to buy one for me, too, as I had such a big and warm heart. I burst into tears and told her they were tears of gladness and gratitude as she had read my mind that I wanted one so much. We both cried, and she knew that Saint Thérèse had "truly spoken" to her because of my emotional and grateful reaction.

At that moment, the crowd gave a spontaneous sigh from the crowd as the priest announced that the service would be delayed for another hour to allow the many people in line to pass Saint Thérèse's relics and pay their respects. My new friend grabbed my arm, squeezed it, and said something very quickly in Portuguese that I did not understand. And then she disappeared again.

About forty-five minutes later, I saw her again at the front of the line again to pass by Saint Thérèse's relics. She grinned at me from the front of the line, waved with one hand, and held up her scarf joyfully in the other.

I watched as she walked up to Saint Thérèse's relics in that gold and jeweled reliquary house that looked like a Gothic church. My friend knelt, bowed her head, and then touched the reliquary with her scarf and for a few seconds rubbed it briefly back and forth for a few seconds quite tenderly and lovingly.

As she got up from her knees and walked by me, she shot me the hugest grin and held her scarf aloft as she passed by, shaking it, pumping it up and down in the air as if she had just won an Academy Award. It was one of the sweetest things

I had ever seen. She was jubilant. And then just as quickly as she had come into my life, she disappeared into the thousands of women in the church. Though I stayed on another three hours, I never saw her again.

I have thought of this wonderful woman in the Portuguese cathedral many times over the years. I still have the scarf she gave me that day. Every time I hold it, my deep and grateful connection to the heart of this wonderful Portuguese woman comes flooding through my heart.

I can also feel my deep connection to the strength, will and loving spirit of Saint Thérèse that began that day in Portugal. I didn't need to wait in line again to rub my scarf over the relics of Saint Thérèse. I had the profound gift of Saint Thérèse's love and strength willed into my bones through the generous spirit of this Portuguese woman, whose name I shall never know.

Connections can be made in an instant. Imagine if we all took an hour every day to avoid our cell phones, take our noses out of our books and take the time to really pay attention to the people around us.

There are people everywhere we go who can benefit from our smiles, our tiny gifts of kindness, or even something so simple as spontaneously offering to take a person's shopping cart back for them in a supermarket parking lot. It doesn't have to be a grand gesture to connect with another human being or an animal.

My rule of thumb is I believe my heart is the bigger of my two brains. So if my head says go right and my heart says to go left, I go left. No exceptions.

The more I do this, the more tiny miracles show up in my life and the more I am able to lift people's spirits around me like the woman in the Portuguese cathedral lifted mine. Life is full of tiny miracles of connection that we can participate in. Let's all pass on the many blessings we have been given!

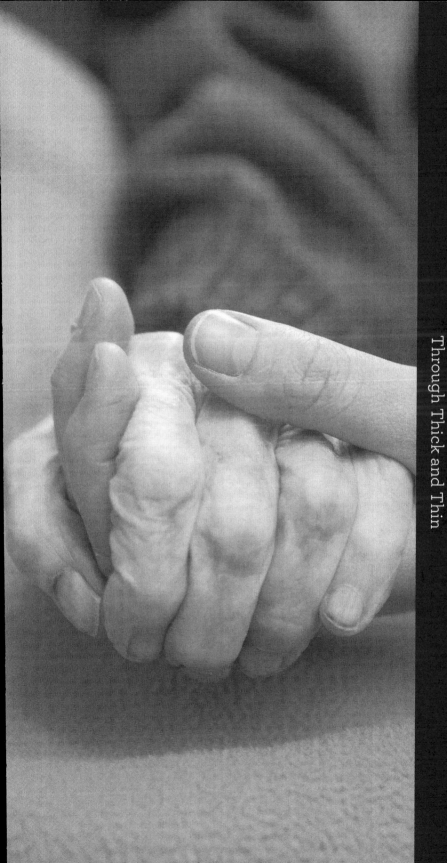

The Psalmist writes, "Trust in God and do good" (Ps. 37:3). This suggests that, as Rabbi David Wolpe says in his book, *Why Faith Matters*, "to do good is to act in harmony with God's design." Poet T. S. Eliot talks about kindness in the form of doing the useful thing: "To do the useful thing, to say the courageous thing, to contemplate the beautiful thing: that is enough for one man's life."

In his poem, "Lines written a few miles above Tintern Abbey," the poet William Wordsworth speaks about the meaning and importance of doing "little, nameless, unremembered acts of kindness and of love" as being a kind of secret joy and far from trivial in importance in our lives and in the lives of others. In fact, Wordsworth goes so far as to say that kindness is a strong influence "on that best portion of a good man's life."

I am deeply grateful for all the countless acts of kindness that I have experienced over the years. Every single gesture of kindness, whether it was practical, courageous, beautiful, simple, loving, or unexpected, has had an incredible influence on my life.

When something difficult happens, most people have that one person in their life they always call first, usually a friend or a family member. The person I have always called first to share news, when I needed some trustworthy advice, or if something unexpectedly went sideways in my life is my closest friend Kath. We have known each other since childhood and have spent countless hours on the phone, at all hours of the day or night, exchanging both the joy and heartbreak in our lives. Her constant refrain to me over the years has been, "I love you and I'm here for you. No matter what." She has been true to her words, through thick and thin, which has been a profound kindness in my life.

After I moved to New York to pursue my dream of being on Broadway, my friend and roommate, Cyndi, would always leave fun notes and delicious treats out on the table in our kitchen for me to discover when I came home from working late. I did the same for her in return. One night when she was out, I created a life-sized person made out of fresh fruit and kitchen utensils, and left it on her bed. When she came home that night, I pretended to be asleep as I listened to her squeal of, "Oh my gosh, what has MA done now?" These secret "little, nameless exchanges" that Cyndi and I shared always felt full of love, whimsical kindness, and frivolity.

My friend Meg, a tried-and-true New Yorker, helped Manhattan become my town, too. Meg and I met when I was born and she worked as an executive assistant to my father at his office in San Francisco. When I was old enough, I would come to the office with my dad. I always made a beeline straight for Meg's office. She would prop me up on a pillow on a big chair and let me type right alongside her. I felt ever so grown up, and I wanted to be just like Meg: kind, loving, gentle, with sparkly eyes and an easy laugh. Meg was the first person to tell me that I "could do anything I set my mind to." When I first moved to New York, Meg let me sleep on her couch until I could find a place of my own. For decades, Meg has always saved a place for me, both in her heart and on her couch, for decades. Yes, kindness can come in the form of a huge heart, a typewriter, and a really comfy couch, too.

My friend Laurie drove and cooked for me throughout my breast cancer radiation treatments. And even though she had her own family to care for, she moved into my home for a while to take care of me when I was operated on for my fifth cancer. Since this cancer was very near my right eye, Laurie stayed by me every moment, even when I had to go through a second surgery to repair the large hole in my face that the first cancer surgery had left behind. When I cried and complained, "I look like I've been in a prize fight and I got massacred!" Laurie would always smile calmly and say, "Can I get you a cup of tea? How about some cookies? Ice cream, perhaps?" Laurie has always kept my spirits up, my body strong, and my pots filled with living plants and colorful flowers, which have always helped me face any difficult time.

My friend Susan was the very first person I met in Seattle. Susan and I met while pushing our children on the swings in Madison Park. After a few minutes of conversation, we were somehow profoundly bonded as deeply as any sisters, and we have remained so since 1992. More than anyone else, Susan helped me make Seattle my new home, where I have lived now for almost twenty years. Susan, who I know from personal experience, is definitely not an early morning person, selflessly offered to drive me to the 7:30 a.m. Friday radiation treatments. Even though Susan lives far on the other side of town, she would always show up at my home on time, with a smile and my favorite coffee for the road: a vanilla latte. Our talks during those early morning drives gave me strength, and Susan's sweet and sassy kindness totally filled my cup, both literally and figuratively.

Sometimes acts of kindness can leave you positively breathless. Sandy walked up to me after I had delivered a speech in church about my cancer experience in church and said, "I was so deeply moved by your speech. What do you need and how can I help?" At first, not knowing Sandy at all, I was shocked by her generous offer. I was so stunned that a complete stranger would offer this that I honestly was at a total loss for words. Then, seeing her face so full of obvious sincerity, I shared with her that what I really needed was more help driving to my many cancer treatments, since I was actually fighting two different cancers at the same time. Without hesitation, Sandy said cheerfully, "I would be happy to drive you! How about two days a week?" This selfless offer of kindness from a total stranger simply amazed me. However, as I got to know Sandy, I understood that this was her unique faith in action: to love and be kind wherever she felt that she was most needed.

Another extraordinary kindness came into my life in the form of cooking lessons. I'm a real "foodie" by nature, and I absolutely love a beautifully cooked meal. One day, I happened to mention to my friend, Lisa, "It's so weird, Lisa. Nothing tastes good to me anymore since I was diagnosed with cancer. I think that I have lost my taste for food." Lisa, who was at that time the chef du cuisine at the prestigious, five-star Herbfarm Restaurant here in Woodinville, Washington (and has since moved on to open her own incredible restaurant, Allium, on Orcas Island) snapped into action. She began coming to my home every Tuesday, on her one day off, to cook a very special lunch—in my kitchen, just for me. The day before she came, Lisa would call and ask me not only what I would like to eat, but also what I would like to learn to cook. Lisa somehow knew that despite my lack of taste for food at that time, the cooking lessons would hook me for sure.

The next day, Lisa would arrive with bags of groceries, and soon my home would be filled with the aroma of all kinds of delicious things cooking, both requested and not. Suddenly, I would be filled with a deep, instinctual longing to eat, which at that time felt like a miracle.

We also had a lot of laughs in my kitchen as I tried to master her professional chef techniques. It's a lot harder than it looks, I can tell you that! I must say all this was an extraordinary kindness, as Lisa's visits gave me something to really look forward to in weeks that were otherwise filled with countless cancer treatments, tremendous pain, and complete exhaustion. Tuesdays quickly became the very best day of my week. And now, finally, thanks to Lisa, I know how to prep and cook a perfect rack of lamb, one of my most favorite foods on earth.

Kindness can come in many forms. My friend Louise is an extraordinary sculptor. She called me on the phone one day and shouted, "I've captured your spirit in bronze! You must come to the studio today! Go get in your car right now!" When I got to the studio, there was a life-sized statue of a woman with a serene smile, both her hands thrown up high into the air as if in exultation and gratitude, and her hair flying wild. "So, what do you think?" Louise asked curiously. "I tried really hard to capture that giant brain of yours going in all directions at the same time!"

I had a smile on my face from ear to ear as I said, "It's definitely me. And she also has breasts that will never sag. That's a definite added bonus! Thanks!"

"Well," Louise said, "I've decided to call her, Mary Anne." I bought the statue on the spot for my fortieth birthday.

And it wasn't just women who have shown me profound kindness over the years. Richard, a dear friend from high school, flew up from California just to mow my lawn, fix all the things in my house that were broken, and help me finish painting my kitchen. Now that's a kind and good friend.

My friend, Derek, an extraordinary graphic artist and painter, flew here to give me painting lessons and then showed his kindness by painting a portrait of me so vibrant in spirit, I often look at it whenever I feel lost. I have that portrait on my wall in my home now, and everyone who sees it says, "Wow. Whoever did that portrait of you really knows you." Both Derek's portrait and Louise's statue always remind me of who I am. That's how it is with kind and good friends. They really know you and what you most need and they show it in all different kinds of ways.

My client, Tony, held his international telecom meetings in my dining room while taking turns with Laurie to dress my surgery wounds. When I first asked Tony why in the world, with his incredibly busy international schedule of travel and work, he would offer to come and help me, he replied matter-of-factly, "Mary Anne. This is what friends do. Get over it!" Tony was the first to see my face after the plastic surgery bandages came off. There was a brief pause and then he said, "Well, dear, you look like the Bride of Frankenstein, but it'll only get better from here on out. More Percocet?"

At two times in my life, my friends Billie and Tim and also Harlan took me into their homes and watched over me while both my body and my spirit healed. Sometimes selfless and devoted acts of kindness such as these truly transcend words.

For years, my friend Tom has left buckets—and I mean buckets—of flowers from his garden on my doorstep. He knows how much I adore flowers and that flowers will always cheer me up, no matter what. Whenever Tom arrives with flowers, I run out of vases.

Over the years, my friend Janaki has just listened, without saying a word. Her kindness has taught me how to honor my own tears and has also freed me to feel loved despite my chaos. Janaki's kindness is not simply listening, but rather one of listening with her whole heart, without judgment or trying to "fix" anything. This kind of listening is exactly what most all of us need, and especially in moments of great suffering or despair. Ultimately, being deeply listened to reminds us of who we truly are and also helps us find faith in our own ability to recover.

My experiences of kindness have taught me that a word, a gesture, or a friend just being there with us as a witness to the many twists and turns of our lives, always contains the potential to transform how we feel. And even if being around kind friends doesn't change how we may feel at any given moment, it's really nice just to have their good company as we face whatever comes—together.

From Me
To You...

Even the simplest act of smiling at a stranger on the street can become a pure, unexpected, random act of kindness. Think for a moment. Who in your life needs a word or gesture of kindness from you today? When you figure that out, then simply be kind in whatever way feels most natural to you.

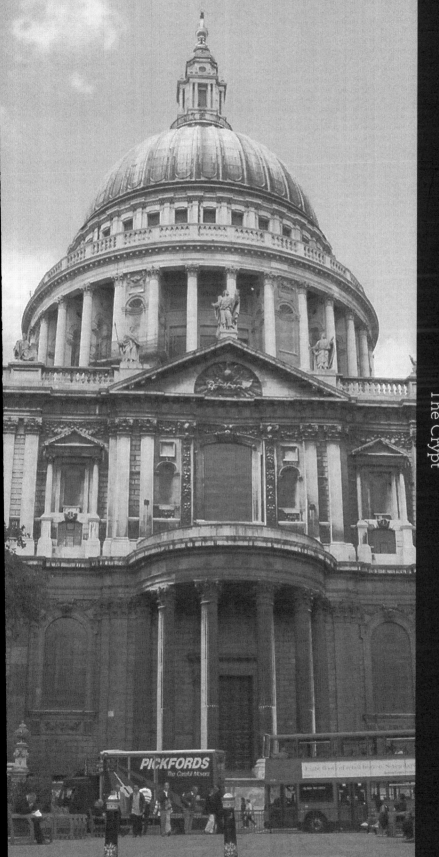

Acceptance

The Crypt

When my first son died, I entered a place of deep darkness, despair, and pain. One day, I dragged myself out of bed and went to see a therapist. After listening to my many reasons for why my life was over, he said, "You know, Mary Anne, people really don't want to kill themselves. What they really want is to be out of pain."

I couldn't have agreed more. Pain was my issue, and at that moment, I saw no way out of it.

I had left my successful acting career to focus on having a child, and I had failed. A miscarriage and then a full-term, stillborn child who we named McKenzie had left me in profound emotional uncertainty, not to mention physical pain. For weeks, I had to wear the very tight binding Ace-bandage-type wrap around my chest, so that my breast milk would not come in. Day and night, this tight binding kept my heart in a vice and was a constant physical reminder of my agony. I was so swollen inside with suffering, it felt like I was wearing a too-tight suit. At any moment, I was sure my body was going to burst "ker-splat" all over the walls like in some alien movie. Some days, it was all I could do to just take another breath, and each breath felt like I was sucking in shards of glass.

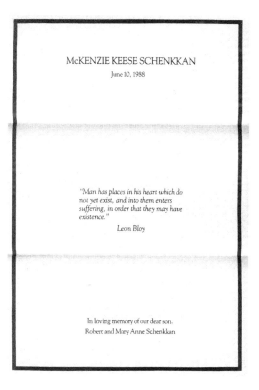

McKENZIE KEESE SCHENKKAN
June 10, 1988

"Man has places in his heart which do not yet exist, and into them enters suffering, in order that they may have existence."
Leon Bloy

In loving memory of our dear son.
Robert and Mary Anne Schenkkan

After McKenzie's funeral, my father called me on the phone. He said, "Mary Anne, I can't bring your son back. But I can send you on a trip anywhere you would like to go in the world. I hope the trip will help you with your healing is some small way." This trip was one of the nicest things my father ever did for me. McKenzie's funeral had used up all of our savings. I was deeply grateful to my father for his gift of a change of scenery. I chose England, Scotland, and Ireland. It was my hope that by returning to the land of my ancestors, I could find healing for my broken heart and tortured soul.

Less than a week into the trip, my hormones crashed, and I just could not stop crying. Through my tears, that same bleak, dark feeling of just wanting to die and be out of all this unbearable pain kept calling. After breakfast one morning, I forced myself out of the hotel and willed myself toward Saint Paul's Cathedral nearby, hoping to find some comfort there.

As I walked around the cathedral, I felt a sense of extreme cold. I was at my lowest ebb. I simply wanted to crawl into a crypt and never be seen again. With my mind and heart in a kind of haze, I just kept forcing my feet to walk around the cathedral, one step at a time, feeling profoundly forlorn, alone, and hopeless. Somehow the voice of my therapist—"Just take it one day at a time," "Keep taking slow, deep breaths no matter how bad it gets," and "You *will* get through this. I promise you,"—all drifted back to my mind while I wandered.

As I walked, my head was down and my eyes gazed at the marble designs in the floor. Suddenly, I had a very strong impulse to look up from the floor. It was strange. It felt as if I'd heard the words, "Mary Anne, look up *now!*" being shouted in my ears. I stopped and when I looked up and turned around, I noticed that no one was standing anywhere close to me. Who had said that?

Again I heard, "Mary Anne, turn around and look up! Straight in front of you." I thought for a second that I might be truly going crazy, but as I lifted my gaze and turned, I noticed that I was standing right in front of Henry Scott Holland's crypt. Henry Scott Holland was a man who had been the canon for that cathedral three hundred years earlier.

I began to read what was written on the front of his crypt:

Death is nothing at all
I have only slipped away into the next room
I am I and you are you
Whatever we were to each other
That we are still
Call me by my old familiar name
Speak to me in the easy way you always used
Put no difference into your tone
Wear no forced air of solemnity or sorrow
Laugh as we always laughed
At the little jokes we always enjoyed together
Play, smile, think of me, pray for me
Let my name be ever the household word that it always was

Let it be spoken without effort
Without the ghost of a shadow in it
Life means all that it ever meant
It is the same as it ever was
There is absolute unbroken continuity
What is death but a negligible accident?
Why should I be out of mind
Because I am out of sight?
I am waiting for you for an interval
Somewhere very near
Just around the corner
All is well
Nothing is past; nothing is lost
One brief moment and all will be as it was before
How we shall laugh at the trouble of parting when we meet again!

—Canon Henry Scott-Holland, 1847–1918, Canon of St. Paul's
   Cathedral

I could not believe it. For the first time since McKenzie's death, I felt a tiny ray of light pierce my deep inner darkness. I read the epitaph again, especially at the end: "All is well. Nothing is past; nothing is lost. One brief moment and all will be as it was before. How we shall laugh at the trouble of parting when we meet again!" I smiled. Then I actually laughed. This was a miracle: I realized that I had not laughed in two months. A wonderful, extraordinary inspiration was right in front of me just when I needed it.

But who had told me to look up? I was still very much alone in front of that crypt. Or was I? It was as if McKenzie was talking to me from beyond the grave: "Mom, you have to get a hold of yourself here. All is well. This is all in order. We actually planned it this way. You have simply forgotten. I am only in the next room waiting for you. All is well. You will get through this. You must. There are others coming after me in this life who will need your love and guidance."

That's when I started laughing even harder. And then came my tears through my laughter. Tears of gratitude. Of joy. Of acceptance. In a blinding flash, I knew I was going to make it. I also absolutely "knew," from a very deep soulful place within me, and without a shadow of a doubt, that there would be other children coming to me.

I also knew where I was headed. I bought a postcard in the cathedral and sent it to my gynecologist, Uzzi, in Los Angeles. It read: "Positive visualization has begun. We will be delivering a baby together soon! I know it!"

I did not know it at the time, but I was actually already pregnant again with my daughter, Sarah. She was born exactly nine months after our trip. The moment of her birth truly felt like a miracle. As she and I locked eyes, there was a profound moment of grace and awe as I said out loud, "Oh look! She's *alive!*" Three years later, our son Joshua was born, and his birth was another profound moment of joy for me. And every time I look at my children, I am reminded of what a joyous miracle of faith and determination they are and how grateful I am for their presence in my life.

Whatever method of inquiry or observation we choose, we always have the potential to shift into a new understanding and acceptance about whatever we are going through. This allows us to be open to the many gifts or tiny miracles that come to us along the way, including, potentially, a new understanding and acceptance of ourselves.

I believed at the time of McKenzie's death that I would never recover. Ever. But my experience of my son's life and death have changed my life forever and shown me that we all have far more strength than we think we do in our times of pain and despair.

Here are some of the lessons I learned from my son's death:

1. No matter how things or our feelings about our circumstances may appear at any given moment in our lives, the old saying "This, too, shall pass" is really true. This applies equally to what we have defined as "positive" or "negative." Any experience or feeling will, and eventually does, pass, no matter how agonizing or blissful.

2. The less attached we are to holding on to any feeling or experience, the faster it will pass. And whatever we resist, hangs on longer. So we need to learn to let go. And the first step towards letting go,

as my dear friend and minister Eric says often, is to "Take a deep breath!" Even if it feels like you are inhaling shards of glass, it will get easier.

3. If we say to ourselves in the split-second spaces between our thoughts, "Who is it that is observing all this drama in our lives?", we discover that we are not, in fact, who we thought we were. We are, each of us, so much more. Spacious. Peaceful. Loving. Wise. Content.

4. The more we stop, close our eyes, and allow the wise "Eternal Observer" part of ourselves to guide our understanding beyond the here-and-now, the more aware we become that we are not just a collection of thoughts, feelings, and experiences. We can let go and trust that we are a much larger spiritual being and remember that each human experience comes with countless potential blessings.

From Me
To You...

If we get stuck, we can always turn to some of our great teachers alive today—such as Byron Katie—and ask ourselves the questions that she teaches called "The Work":

Is it true? Can you absolutely know that it's true? How do you react, what happens, when you believe that thought? Who would you be without the thought?

For more information on Byron Katie, go to:
www.thework.com/thework-4questions.php

Her books:
Who Would You Be Without Your Story?
A Thousand Names for Joy

Rise

Living from a Higher Perspective

As a young child, whenever I was having a bad day or I complained that someone had done something mean to me, my mother would always smile and say, "Rise above it!"

Sometimes when I vehemently complained that her "rise above it" strategy was not working (or even realistic), my mother would take the opposite angle and would say, "Well, then you certainly don't have to stoop down to their level."

As I got a little older, I decided that both her "rise" and "stoop" strategies were a total cop-out.

If rising above something meant going numb, and somehow letting the other person off the hook without any responsibility for their actions, then she could just forget it. Was I supposed to go numb to the fact that another person was a total jerk or had gone out of their way to personally insult me? Was I supposed to go numb to the fact that someone had beaten me at something and they had cheated? Was I supposed to go numb to the fact that I didn't get into the college I wanted or get the boyfriend or job I wanted? No way.

Even if I couldn't change my negative circumstances, my getting angry and thinking about somehow getting even at least felt like I was not letting her, him, them, it, whatever it was, beat me. Then I heard a sermon one Sunday entitled, "The Moth on the Persian Rug." One day, this moth fluttered down from the sky and landed on a Persian rug. He landed first in the blue section of the rug and soon he became very depressed and sad. Then he fluttered a bit and landed in a part of the rug that was yellow. His spirits began to lift, and he perked up. In fact, his spirits perked up so much that he waltzed right into a red section of the rug. Here he began to feel angry and aggressive, stamping his little moth feet. He marched along until he found himself in a white section, and instantly he shifted into an extremely peaceful and serene mood. He stayed here awhile, for this peace felt very good.

But when he got up and got moving again, he walked into the black section of the rug. Soon, he felt totally lost and frightened in the dark. He wanted to get out of the black darkness, but he had no idea how. Eventually, he found his way out of the black, and wandered into the green section of the rug. He felt very at ease, and it reminded him of the trees he had slept in at night before he had landed in this color nightmare of a place.

This moth kept moving around and around on the Persian rug, falling into this color and that, provoking this emotion or that, until he became just so exhausted he simply stopped, lay down, closed his little moth eyes, and let go. It felt good to let go of always being at the mercy of the color he was in. He had a dream that night that he could fly.

Eventually the moth woke up and remembered from the dream that he knew how to fly. He began to slowly flutter his wings. Soon, he lifted off the Persian rug, and up, up, up he rose, into the air. Eventually he was high enough to see where he was and where he had been. Looking down, he saw how incredibly beautiful the rug was, seen from this larger, higher perspective. He also remembered all those separate colors and different moods. That memory made him a little nauseous and unsettled. "Why couldn't I see all this when I was down there?" he wondered.

The story's conclusion was that if the moth had only known from the beginning to rise high above the rug to see its larger design, he would have been able to see that he had never been trapped at all, ever, for any moment. He could have flown free at any time, he just didn't know that he had that ability at the time. But he created the feeling of being trapped in all of those different emotions, in reaction to simple colors; it had always been a Persian rug, and nobody had forced him to feel anything.

But it was equally true that his discovery of total and complete freedom was all a part of the Grand Design, if only the little moth had just been able to see it.

I realized this all sounded very familiar. In a blinding flash of the obvious, I finally understood the perspective my mother had been trying to teach me all my life. If each of us could rise high above and see our lives in a larger perspective of a greater spiritual whole, we know that we always have total freedom in how we respond, react, or feel in any given moment or with any person who crosses our path. We would also know that we are never trapped by any given circumstance, or emotion. It is always our choice.

To "rise above" anything, in any given moment is to see the person, the event, or circumstance from the highest point of wisdom that we are capable of. If we "stoop" to the lowest level of any given circumstance, we totally lose our perspective.

It wasn't until after her death in my adult years that I was able to see how wise my mother had truly been. I wish I had been able to tell my mother while she was alive how much her perspective on daily life now means to me and how grateful I am to her every day. But during my youth and young adulthood, I was not able to rise above anything, and so I could not see my relationship with her with a very clear perspective or vision.

Yet I am sure that if she were alive today, my mother would say that my finally learning the true meaning of her words was all part of the perfect timing in the Grand Design of my life. I'm sure she would also laugh with me at the silliness of my beating myself up for taking so long to understand what she meant. There is never, ever one moment lost or wasted or that is not part of our spiritual growth.

We all wander and travel the world in search of The Truth, when The Truth is always there, right under our noses and in our hearts, all along, from the very beginning of time. All we have to do is rise above ourselves to see our lives with greater clarity and perspective. And we can fly to freedom any time we wish.

From Me
To You...

My favorite book of all is Paulo Coelho's *The Alchemist*. It is a charming tale and one I have read over and over again through the years. It always makes my spirits rise every time I read it. The Alchemist was originally written in Portuguese and has since been translated into sixty-seven languages, winning the Guinness World Record for most translated book by a living author, and it has sold more than 65 million copies in more than 150 countries, becoming one of the best-selling books in history.

The Alchemist tells the journey of a young Andalusian shepherd boy named Santiago. Santiago, believing a recurring dream he has to be prophetic, decides to travel to the pyramids of Egypt to find his treasure. On the way, he encounters love, danger, opportunity, and disaster, and learns a lot about himself and the impact he has on the people he meets, just by being himself.

One of the significant characters that he meets is an old king named Melchizedek, who tells him, "When you want something, all the universe conspires in helping you to achieve it." This is essentially the core philosophy of the book. During his travels, Santiago meets a beautiful Arabian woman named Fatima who explains to him that if he follows his heart, he shall find what it is he seeks. And when Santiago finally meets the Alchemist, he truly understands his teachings. The book is incredibly inspirational, unexpectedly amazing and deeply reassuring all at the same time. I hope it lifts your spirits as much as it has mine.

Integrity

A Bundle of Life

Are there any of us who truly live up to our expectations? I believe that integrity is the bedrock of life and work. The word *integrity* stems from the Latin adjective *integer*, which means "whole or complete." Acquiring a sense of "inner wholeness" is as simple as following through with our professed morality. By behaving in accordance with our belief system, we achieve personal integrity, as solid as the foundation of a skyscraper. I learned another description of living with full integrity from my dear friends Mark and Terri. Mark and his wife, Terri, both have tremendous personal and professional integrity, and they introduced me to a classical perspective on integrity from South Africa, called *Ubuntu*. Translated from Zulu, *Ubuntu* means, "My humanity is inextricably bound up in yours..."

Or, as Mark would say:
We belong in a bundle of life.
A person is human through other people within community.
I am human because I share; I belong; I participate...
We are diminished when others are humiliated or oppressed.
To forgive is not just altruistic; rather, it is the best form of self-assurance. It gives people resilience; and allows them to emerge still human despite all efforts to dehumanize them.

Ubuntu teaches that the rewards of integrity benefit the entire community, but its the qualities can also be applied in our quest for personal integrity:

> Generosity
> Openness
> Belonging
> Participation
> Caring
> Sharing
> Friendliness
> Approachability
> Affirmation
> Encouragement
> Self-confidence
> Forgiveness
> Reconciliation

Just as the positive aspects of an *Ubuntu* community can foster personal integrity, traits that oppose it can halt a search for inner wholeness in its tracks:

Anger
Blame
Fault-finding
Resentment
Vengefulness
Cut-throat tactics

Ubuntu was the underlying concept employed by South African President Nelson Mandela in establishing the Truth and Reconciliation Commission following independence in the mid-1990s, which provided amnesty to those individuals (government officials, military, police, etc.), *despite* the atrocities

it had unleashed on the blacks in South Africa. The Truth and Reconciliation Commission was not a war-crimes tribunal, but rather a forum for the public admission of crimes to those victimized, a process by which aggressors and victims alike could heal from the damage done by apartheid. By choosing to avert vengeance in favor of fostering a true, *Ubuntu*-based community, President Mandela avoided the bloodshed typical in other African countries transitioning from colonial, minority control.

Ever since I heard the principles of *Ubuntu*, I have been trying to live them and take them into every situation, both personally and professionally. It feels like a more openhearted, inclusive way of focusing my energy and time. But, while I aspire to be a person of integrity, I don't always reach anywhere near my high expectations, or *Ubuntu*, for that matter. Over and over, I've caught myself reaching for a kind of perfectionism that was highly unrealistic, which left me with a constant sense of failure and a feeling of not measuring up. I think that I have used the guise of aspiring to be "perfect" to cover a lack of understanding about what living in true "integrity" means. It seems that I am struggling just like everyone else just to find my way in the world and to do the right thing. Perhaps when it comes to integrity, or *Ubuntu*, that is the very best any of us can aspire to.

I turned to Mark for advice on this question. I asked him, "What do we do when we don't measure up to our own high expectations, or we fail to execute along the principles of *Ubuntu?*"

Mark responded: "Here are some thoughts…"

> There is no hypocrisy in falling short; we are all human and fail daily (in all aspects of our lives) to live up to the potential of our higher calling and commitment to the integrity and principles we hold dear…

> When we fail, the way forward, is to be honest, humbly forthcoming and transparent in acknowledging when we fall short and openly asking for forgiveness. It is in the lack of transparency, in the excuse-making, in the "cover up," or in the non-acknowledgement or non-forgiveness seeking, that others can earnestly perceive us as being a hypocrite. That's not to say that we can overcome every situation with every person. With some, after we do our part, it will translate or evolve into the question of "who owns the problem," as they may be influenced by other issues, over which we have little or no control or causal responsibility…

> And, as you shared, it is our responsibility to get up fresh each morning, giving ourselves permission to start anew…

> —Blessings, Mark

I decided to make my own list of what integrity meant to me and how successful I believed I actually was in living up to it.

Living with integrity means:
In life, work, and play, I try my best to do the right thing, to the best of my ability, at all times.

Upon further self-examination, I decided that to expect myself to do the right thing to the best of my ability at all times was an unrealistic expectation and too much pressure.

I learn from every experience.

This is a reasonable expectation. However, I don't always learn my lesson immediately and I sometimes have to make the same mistake several times before I "get it," but I do keep trying.

I try to listen to others from my deepest self in order to make the best decision possible.

Truth is, at times, I actually interrupt people when they are talking, don't listen, and don't make the best decision possible as a result.

I am not afraid to admit a mistake and change a decision when I discover that it is wrong or it is not for the highest and greatest good for all involved.

Actually, I tend to be afraid of making mistakes or making the wrong decision and somehow causing harm to others. I don't always act in the highest or greatest good for all, even when I try. This was upsetting when I realized it.

I try to be honest, but never unkind, to my children, my friends, my clients, and myself.

I think I do a better job with others than with myself.

I try to treat people with the respect and kindness that they deserve.

The honest truth is that I am often in such a hurry or so distracted, that I cannot always do this. But when I do make the time, keep my awareness open, and live with a kind heart, my life is enriched by encounters with people in all kinds of places that I never would have imagined.

I always try to help make it possible for each person I work with to discover and celebrate their strengths, explore and resolve their blind spots, and then give the very best speech or presentation they are capable of.

This is true. I take my work and my responsibility to my clients very seriously.

I try to rise to my fullest potential and then transform the world to the best of my ability.

Sometimes the world and the people in it really don't want me to transform them as much as I might think they do. I see now that the world would be better served if I made peace within myself and brought that peaceful me everywhere I go, rather than driving myself into the ground and telling others what to do.

I am willing to admit and apologize when I have not lived up to any of these principles.

Truth be told, sometimes I really believe I am right and this blinds me to what others think or might be feeling and how they might actually have an even better solution to a given problem.

For me, the journey of improving my integrity remains ongoing. What does integrity mean to you?

Responsibility

A Cautionary Tail

One of the most irresponsible things I have done in my life was buying two puppies, at the same time, in a moment of weakness. When I think back on it all now, I wonder how it was possible that I didn't see that this was a very, very bad idea. But in hindsight, I recognize that I have often done things I later wished I had done differently, and that as Auguste Rodin said, "Nothing is a waste of time if you use the experience wisely." Well after I realized my mistake, re-homing these two puppies taught me several valuable lessons.

*****

It all started when my son Joshua came to me and said, "Hey, Mom. I'm going to be going to college next year, and it'll be awfully quiet around here. I really think you're going to need some company. I've got a great idea. What do you think about getting a pair of puppies?"

There was a long silence as my mind began to flash wildly in all directions. All I could think of was, *Two puppies? Are you kidding? Oh no. The responsibility. The work. The mess. The mud. The chewing. The digging. The picking up poop day in and day out. The vet bills...*

Biscuit, our field-champion, chocolate Labrador retriever, had recently passed away. We were all devastated when she was diagnosed with kidney cancer and had to be put down after every measure had been taken to heal and save her.

Joshua was still standing there staring at me, waiting for an answer. "Mom? You're awfully quiet."

I snapped out of the chaos in my head, "Oh, sorry, Joshua. I'll give your idea some serious thought, OK? I'll let you know in a few days, after I've had some time to think about it."

In hindsight, I know that if I had truly listened to my instincts at that very instant, I would have acknowledged that my gut reaction was right on, and the entire affair would have ended there. Oh, but it didn't.

Lesson #1: Listen to your gut.

Suddenly there was this kind of "doggie nostalgia" kicking in. Images from the ten years of Biscuit's life began ricocheting through my mind and heart. *Biscuit was so cute as a puppy. Wasn't she fun? Didn't she leap six feet in the air*

every time I said the word "walk?" Wasn't she the only truly constant and utterly devoted companion in my life for the past ten years? Suddenly, all the work involved disappeared from my thoughts.

Joshua began to research dog breeds online. Together, we pored over online photos of puppies from PAWS, dog-rescue organization sites, shelters, and anything else that popped up in the paper.

The more research I did, the more I came back to seriously considering Labrador retrievers. But then, my panic would suddenly return. Not only would both Joshua and Sarah be gone, but also I would be left alone with two puppies, soon to be big, needy, adult dogs, to train and feed and manage on my own. The freedom I now had to come and go as I pleased would be gone. Yikes! I was suddenly right back on top of the fence again, and as much as I missed Biscuit, I realized that I was actually enjoying my freedom since her death. I also realized I wasn't sure I ever wanted the responsibility of a dog again. This emotional rollercoaster should have been a red flag…

Lesson #2: Do not be swayed or make any important decision while in grief or nostalgia over the memory of a recently deceased pet or relative.

At these times like these in my life, the internal voice saying, "Please listen to your gut," and "You must heed your intuition," tried desperately to get my attention. Clearly, this was one of those times and my inner voices were screaming, *NO! Two dogs? Two puppy dogs? Bad idea! Bad, BAD idea. Don't do it! Just back away!*

But did I listen? Nope. I told my negative, inner voices to shut up.

I found a breeder of pure bred hunting labs, and the moment Joshua and I set eyes on these dogs, we were both done for. They were absolutely the most adorable little beings we had ever seen.

I find that we get exactly as many chances to change our minds as we need, even if we wind up scraping the very lowest point before taking the opportunity. In this case, I gave up one of the early, easy chances to heed my inner voices. It was going to be a lot harder to change things from here on out.

Lesson #3: Back to lesson #1.

In less than fifteen minutes, I had picked a chocolate and Joshua, had picked a yellow Lab puppy. Twelve hundred dollars later, we had our two darling puppies, and Joshua was in heaven in the back seat, cuddling both puppies in his lap, with them licking him everywhere they could find a bare spot of flesh until they fell asleep.

About fifteen minutes into the drive, Joshua said, "So, what are you thinking, Mom?"

"Honest?" I asked.

"Yeah, of course, honest."

"Well, Joshua, I'm actually thinking how much responsibility and work this is going to be for at least another ten to twelve years of my life. And how I might just come to hate them, despite how cute they currently are. What are *you* thinking?"

Without hesitation Joshua said, "They're just so cute. I love them so much already. What shall we name them?"

We finally settled on Gus for the chocolate male Lab and Champ for the yellow female Lab. Joshua was stuck on Champ as her name, but secretly, I knew I would be calling her Gracie behind his back.

On the way home, we stopped off at the pet store and bought over five hundred dollars' worth of equipment: crates, food, a plastic puppy pen, toys, treats, things for them to chew on, balls, twisty ropes, rawhide, and Nylabones. I felt like I was outfitting twins: a pink Kong for her, a blue Kong for him.

Spending that much money at the pet store was, in hindsight, a choice I made to somehow fool, or some might say, "trap," myself into being more committed than I actually felt at the time.

Lesson #4: Be honest with yourself.

It was late by the time we finally got home. Since we did not have any way to contain puppies at first and we had to get things set up, we let them both loose in the house while we unloaded everything out of the car and began to set up their puppy pen. Bad idea.

Suddenly our quiet, calm, peaceful house turned into absolute chaos.

It was late. Joshua and I were exhausted and ready for bed. Together, we herded the puppies into their new crate downstairs. We were both beat. As we said goodnight, Joshua patted my shoulder and said, "Everything will be fine in the morning, you'll see, Mom." I nodded and sighed with relief.

That's when the howling began.

Lesson #5: Pay attention to the clues.

As I went downstairs, I thought, "They are going back, no matter how cute they are."

Lesson #6: Do what you say you are going to do.

First thing next morning, when I got them upstairs, they both took off, and ran under the dining room table, and started to pee on my expensive, handmade carpet. "Oh no! Not again!" I yelled. "NO!" I ran over and grabbed both of them by the scruff of their neck and practically threw them out the back door. "Potty out *here!*" I shut the door and crawled under the table to start cleaning.

By this time, Joshua had gotten up and was coming into the kitchen for breakfast. He noticed Gus and Gracie sitting quietly by the back door with their noses pressed to the glass. "Geez, Mom. Look at 'em. Aren't they cute? Mom? Look at 'em!"

I snarled, "Yeah I'll look at 'em again after I have scrubbed this pee out of the rug under the table here. And done their second load of laundry in six hours. Oh, and did I mention, after *you* went to sleep, they pooped all over their crate and I had to clean that again too, along with giving them both a bath? It was a disaster!"

"Geez, Mom. No need to get all passive-aggressive about this. You agreed to this, remember?" Joshua said as he reached into the cabinet for his cereal and a bowl. I thought to myself, *Well, you could offer to help me here. After all, you weren't the one up all night cleaning up after these dogs.* And then my mind switched into everyday reality: Joshua had to hurry now and get out the door since he was late for school. He couldn't possibly help me at that moment, and he was right: I had agreed to this. So, I gritted my teeth and kept silent, or I would have thrown Joshua outside with the dogs, too.

Lesson #7: Hold others accountable.

It was a nice day outside so I decided to take the dogs for a walk. I grabbed the new leashes and said, "Okay, guys. This will be fun! Let's go for a walk!"

Gus trotted happily out the front door but Gracie refused to move. At this moment, with Gus pulling at the end of a twenty-six-foot leash in one direction toward the street and Gracie spread-eagled over the threshold, I felt something snap as my body twisted into a quite unnatural position. I felt a

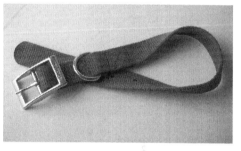

sharp stabbing in my neck, and suddenly I was in terrible pain. I had pinched a nerve. Now I wasn't just frustrated, I was getting mad.

I got about half a block before I realized that this really, *really* wasn't going to work.

Lesson #8: Ignore lessons 1–7 at your own peril.

This was more work than I had ever imagined, and I simply did not have the time or the energy to do this. I had a job, a life, and a future to think about. So I scooped Gracie up, reined Gus in, and marched back home.

I called my vet, and sniveled into the phone with tears streaming down my face, "Is there any place you can, you know, (sniff) send a dog away for a while so they can, you know, (sniff) be trained, and the owner can take a brief vacation from them, and they come back, you know, (sniff) still cute but all trained?"

"How old are they again, and how long have you had them?" the vet assistant chirped into the phone.

"Uh, well, they're eight weeks and they've been with us, uh, less than a day."

The vet assistant laughed out loud, and I suddenly wanted to strangle her, too.

"I see. Well, puppies can be a lot of work for anyone. So don't be too hard on yourself."

The vet assistant gently suggested, "Perhaps you might want to think a little more along the lines of actually re-homing them." I had never heard the term *re-home* before, so I asked, "Does that mean I have to change my house?"

"Actually, re-homing means you find another home for them, so both they and you are more at peace." Later that day, after the breeder refused to take the puppies back, I decided to do just that.

I put an ad on Craigslist and soon found the most amazing homes for both puppies. It was Easter when I drove each puppy to their new owners. On my way home after dropping off each puppy, I knew I was going home to an empty house, and yet my heart was strangely full. When I got home, I opened the door and everything was quiet and clean and in order, just as I had left it.

The responsibility for those two adorable, beautiful puppy beings had passed to two homes, with at least four people in each house to look after them, and it was truly the most responsible choice for me. As I was eating my lunch, I realized that those two puppies had given me a great gift. Their presence had shown me that I now knew I wanted to focus on finding human companionship.

Lesson #9: When you know you have done the wrong thing, take full responsibility for your decision and then solid steps towards fixing it.

Next time, I would follow my own intuition and make a more responsible choice at the very beginning.

Lesson #10: Make a different choice next time!

Lesson #1: Listen to your gut.

Lesson #2: Do not be swayed or make any important decision while in grief over the memory or nostalgia of a recently deceased pet or relative.

Lesson #3: Back to lesson #1.

Lesson #4: Be honest with yourself.

Lesson #5: Pay attention to the clues.

Lesson #6: Do what you say you are going to do.

Lesson #7: Hold others accountable.

Lesson #8: Ignore lessons 1–7 at your own peril.

Lesson #9: When you know you have done the wrong thing, take full responsibility for your decision, and then one solid step towards fixing it.

Lesson #10: Make a different choice next time!

Patience

It's a Virtue, I Hear

W henever life threw me a curveball, or I launched into a tirade about how something did not work out or move fast enough, or I complained that I was just plain unhappy, my grandmother, Nonny, would always say with a sly smile, "Patience is a virtue, I hear!"

Sometimes I just wanted to punch her.

But I did try to take her advice to heart. When there was a delay, I tried to smile through gritted teeth and wait. Other times, I would literally hear Nonny's voice in my head right after I had thrown something across the room in total exasperation, frustration, or anger.

So while I didn't really understand the meaning of "Patience is a virtue, I hear!" early in my life, and that pat phrase definitely infuriated me on more than one occasion growing up, I found that I have returned to it as a constant refrain of wisdom and very important perspective over the years.

But why is patience so tough?

We live in a culture that seems to promise instant gratification. And when things appear to take too long or don't go as fast as we want them to, we get seriously agitated. With a cell phone or computer, any of us can send an e-mail, text, or even a photo to anyone in the world, in an instant. And we get mad when they don't answer us equally fast.

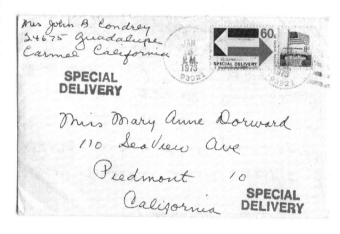

Most of gen X and gen Y grew up with e-mail and texting, with constant and instant access to their friends and family. Those of us in the Baby Boomer or Traditionalist generations still remember getting mail by a stamp, otherwise known as "snail mail," which took days instead of seconds to reach its destination. Now even most of *us* have cell phones and are texting or e-mailing throughout the day. With my two kids being in college, I text them far more than I speak

with them on the phone. Yet text messages and e-mails can only go so far in terms of what the formats themselves allow us to communicate. Overall, we are losing our sense of perspective with regard to patience and time in our everyday life. We are also losing patience with ourselves and how long, realistically speaking, our ideas, hopes, dreams, and goals take to come to fruition. It's as if we have decided that if our dreams don't become a reality in a split second these days, then they are not worth waiting for. As a result, we are giving up on our dreams and our precious potential far too quickly.

From Me
To You...

What dream of your life have you given up on because it did not come to fruition fast enough or because you may have gotten snagged along the way? Take some time now to revisit that dream and see if it is still calling to you for some attention, and if it is, then have patience, go for it, and don't give up until you realize it—no matter how long it takes.

Honesty

The Man at the Bottom of the Barrel

When my kids were young, I took them on a tour of Alcatraz, the former maximum-security prison out in the middle of the San Francisco Bay. We were at the top of the prison, touring the individual cells, when the PA system crackled: "For those of you on the Alcatraz tour today, we have a very special opportunity. Leon 'Whitey' Thompson, one of the only four men who were ever released from Alcatraz prison directly to the San Francisco streets, is here with us today signing his books. If you would like to meet Mr. Thompson, he is on the second floor for the next hour. Feel free to stop by and say hello."

My kids and I looked at each other and said, "Cool! Let's go!" As we stood in line, I suggested that each of us think of a question we would like to ask Mr. Thompson. While we waited, we kept saying, "Wow," since this was such an unusual opportunity to meet someone who had actually been imprisoned here. By the time we got to the head of the line, Mr. Thompson greeted us. He broke the ice by first speaking to me.

"What fine-looking children you have, ma'am," he said politely. Mr. Thompson was not at all the image I had in my mind of an ex-convict. He was well dressed in a suit and in front of him were a stack of his two books, which he was signing and selling that day.

"Thank you very much, Mr. Thompson. I would like to buy both your books, and would you please inscribe them to my children?"

"I would be happy to do that, ma'am. But please, call me Whitey. And what are your children's names?" At that he pulled out one of each book and opened the front covers.

"Mr. Thompson, er, Whitey, their names are Sarah spelled with an *h* and Joshua. Um, while you are doing that, do you mind answering a few questions?" I said, with some hesitation.

Whitey Thompson looked up, put down his pen, and gave us his full, undivided attention. "Of course. I would be happy to answer any questions you have, if I can. What would you like to know?" he said, smiling a warm, genuine smile. He looked back and forth among the three of us. Silence. "Who's first?"

Sarah shook her head rapidly back and forth, lips pursed, signaling a strong "No." I looked at Josh. "Okay, Josh. Your turn. What would you like to ask Mr. Thompson?"

Josh did not miss a beat. "Mr. Thompson. Uh, Whitey, sir. Can you please tell me what possessed you to rob those thirty-nine banks in the first place?"

Whitey smiled a smile at Josh and then at me. "My, he is quite direct, isn't he?"

"Yes, he certainly is," I said, blushing.

"How old are you, son?"

"I'm eight years old, sir. I mean Whitey. So why did you do it? Thirty-nine banks is a lot of banks. I'd really like to know why you did that."

"Well, son, first of all I want you to know that your question is a very good one. And without going into a whole lot of detail, I can tell you that I was in the war and I came out of it a very, very angry man. But I am living proof, son, that you can get to the very bottom of a deep, dark barrel and pull yourself out."

Whitey smiled a very warm smile at Josh and then turned his face to me. "Ma'am?"

I took a deep breath and let out a careful sigh. I wasn't sure how honest I could be with a complete stranger. I had felt very depressed for quite some time, in particular from my recent divorce. I decided to risk it.

"Whitey, as we were walking around, I was listening to the audio program on my headphones that the prison provides for visitors, you know, that tells the history of this place and also has interviews with former prisoners?"

"Yes, ma'am, I know it well," Whitey said with a grin.

"Well, I remember your interview in particular, Whitey. When you came on at one point, you said that when you arrived here at Alcatraz, your 'heart was cold as a stone.'" I looked to him for confirmation.

"Yes ma'am, that was true," Whitey said, without any trace of bitterness.

"Well, Whitey, I have to admit, I am very familiar with that place myself. You know, that 'cold as a stone' place? Well, what I want to know is, do you remember the moment the tide began to turn for you? You know, from cold as a stone to something different?"

Inside I was desperately hoping he could help me do something about the cold stone weighing heavy on my own heart. I hoped that he had some words of wisdom to help me out of the deep solitary confinement I had felt trapped in for some time.

Whitey looked at me with the kindest face and said, "I absolutely do remember that moment, ma'am. It was just about the most important moment of my life. It was the moment I realized that I was the only person who had gotten me in here, and I was the only person who was going to get me out."

He paused. "And after that moment, ma'am, everything, absolutely everything, changed for me. My decision to be really honest with myself and change my focus shifted my entire future. Instead of being angry and bitter and resentful about my past all the time, my entire focus became about what I, personally, was going to do to get me out of here. I began thinking about how I was going to build a different, more productive future for myself. And here I am today. I'm happily married, doing work that I love. I actually created that better life for myself that started here on Alcatraz those many years ago. Who would have thought an inmate from this place would now be a best-selling author? I talk in schools, helping kids stay out of trouble so they never do the kinds of things I did or have to go through what I had to go through. I figured that's the best kind of work I could do now, you know, to help others from my own personal experience. I want kids to stay out of prison."

I was too stunned to speak. But Josh spoke up, "Wow, Whitey. That's so cool. If I wrote you a letter, would you answer it?"

"Of course I would, son. I'm happy to answer any question you have. I'd also be real interested to hear what you honestly think of my books."

Not long after we got home, Josh did write Whitey, and Whitey answered. In fact, Josh and Whitey Thompson kept up a correspondence for several years. I never knew the contents of either Josh's or Whitey's letters. It was private. But what I did notice was that over the next ten years, now and again, I would find Josh in his room reading one of Whitey's books or letters. He is eighteen now, and he still picks up Whitey's books.

Josh wasn't the only one of our family who was deeply moved from the encounter at Alcatraz. The visit had a huge impact on me as well. I kept thinking about what Whitey had said: "I absolutely do remember that moment ma'am.

It was the moment I realized that I was the only person who had gotten me in here, and I was the only person who was going to get me out."

When we met Whitey, I was feeling so stuck, I might as well have been in a prison myself. I imagined that Alcatraz couldn't have been any worse than the cruel and punishing prison that my mind was trapped in. I kept asking myself over and over, "How am I going to get myself out of this? If Whitey could meet and overcome his cold-as-a-stone self on Alcatraz, I sure should be able to do it, too."

Whitey Thompson was right, and he was such an inspiration to me. I realized that I was the only one who had gotten myself into the snarl of anger and rage and frustration with my life. I was the only one who could place myself in a new environment where I could get help and support to honestly face my anger and myself. I was the only one who could do the necessary work to get to the other side of my issues and then get past them and move on to live a healthy and happy life. In dealing with healing the pain of my life, honesty with myself was the best policy.

However, I think asking or expecting ourselves to be completely honest every second of the day is somewhat unrealistic, much as I personally hate to admit that. I know there are those who believe that brutal honesty no matter where the chips may fall or who gets hurt, is the only way to go. I disagree. I think there are times and situations where complete honesty is not the best policy, especially when it comes to hurting another person's feelings. Some of our truth is better left unsaid when it comes to others' lives or their children's lives.

Honesty with ourselves is another matter. I believe that being truly brutally honest with oneself can, if tempered with compassion, be extremely healing and transformative. The only problem is that we are often most critical of and hardest on ourselves. This, unfortunately, warps our ability to see ourselves clearly, and then our brutal honesty becomes misguided. So being brutally honest with ourselves can be a bit slippery and tricky to accomplish well.

When unexpected people cross our path and show us what brutal honesty with ourselves actually looks like, and then we see how brutal honesty has shifted their worlds completely, we feel graced and inspired by their hard-earned wisdom. Leon "Whitey" Thompson inspires in all of us the ability to recognize our capacity to rethink our choices and to see how our new choices can significantly impact the future direction of our lives.

During the writing of this book, when I tried to reach Leon "Whitey" Thompson to thank him again for his words, which had so profoundly changed my life, I learned that he had died of congestive heart failure in 2005 at the age of eighty-three.

His books and music are:

Last Train to Alcatraz:
The Autobiography of Leon (Whitey) Thompson

Rock Hard: Autobiography of
Former Alcatraz Inmate Leon "Whitey" Thompson

Unfinished Tattoo (music)

Change

The Beauty of Difference

The Buddha said, "Change your thoughts and you change your world." Changing our thoughts can really help us as we watch the realities of our body, our perceptions, and our self-expression change. Sometimes this can feel like watching a train wreck. We are transfixed and yet horrified by the inevitability of change. But we can choose to accept the change, to look with wonder instead of horror. The words we choose to describe our thoughts, ourselves, and our internal and external realities will help us interpret the meaning of these changes.

In his book, *A Long Walk to Freedom*, Nelson Mandela talks a lot about change. In fact, he says, "There is nothing like returning to a place that remains unchanged to find the ways in which you yourself have altered." Nothing ever stays the same. In fact, the only constant in this world is change. How we embrace or resist these changes makes all the difference between a life of resistance and a life of acceptance.

In learning how to weather our internal and external changes gracefully, we can learn how to develop a gentle but unshakable composure. Our confidence in ourselves will grow, and we will become so much more at peace being our True Self. As our True Self shines, and we realize the real truth of life, we become so much more radiant. True compassion begins to naturally radiate out from us, and this brings delight and comfort to others.

Recently, I went to Carmel-by-the-Sea, California where I spent many summers as a child. When I was young, it was a huge, long, beautiful beach. On my recent trip, the beach seemed so much smaller, and it didn't take me nearly as long to walk it from end to end as I had remembered. The shapes of the rocks at either end of the beach also seemed different than I had remembered. Over the years since my last visit, the waves had lashed at the rocks, sculpting and eroding them. Yet while the shapes of the rocks were different than I had remembered, they were as beautiful as ever—just different.

From Me
To You...

Here is one of my most favorite quotes of all:

"The truth consists of creating an outlet so that the imprisoned splendor may escape."—Robert Browning

If we looked at the changes of our lives this way—change as an imprisoned splendor just waiting to escape—how might we live our lives differently? Would we embrace change more willingly and with a greater sense of curiosity?

Beyond the Horizon

"You don't have to be something. You just have to *be*." Those words came to me as a constant refrain from New York acting teacher and Actors Studio founder Lee Strasberg. Learning to just be, trusting I am more than enough just as I am, onstage or off, has been one of the most challenging lessons of my life. In fact, I'm still learning.

It's been thirty years since I studied with Lee Strasberg, had an acting career, and performed on Broadway and TV in New York. Leaving my acting career was a challenging decision. But I wanted to have children, and having children was, for me, more important than any career ever could be. I also knew far too many people in my profession who never put their children to bed at night, and that was not a price I was willing to pay. So I quit my career and put the full force (some might call it obsession) of my being into having and raising my children. This year, my daughter and son are both in college, and that cycle of child rearing has come to a close.

But then, as in all cycles of nature, there was a rebirth: Me! Finally, after all these years, I made time to write this book, a new birth. Now the writing of my book is also coming to a close, which is a kind of symbolic death. Yet the rebirth will come as I begin to meet all the people who have read my book, and go on tour and give speeches. So this book actually is a birth, death, and rebirth cycle in my life, practically all at once!

I have noticed many birth, death, and rebirth cycles over the course of my life. My son, brother, mother, grandparents, aunt, dog, and canaries have all died. As my memory traces over each of these beings' influence on my life, a saying comes to mind: "Man has places in his heart which do not yet exist, and into them enters suffering, in order that they may have existence." I miss them all and am so grateful that each of them crossed my path for a time, but I have moved on to embrace new people to love and new experiences to cherish. This is not to say I have ever forgotten any of them. Quite the contrary. I bless all of them each and every day for what I have learned from them about love and the wisdom of living.

This cycle of rebirth is true for other relationships, such as friendships, family, or lovers—even my marriage. I am truly grateful for each person, whether he or she came into my life for a day, a season, or a lifetime. No matter how hard, how confusing, or how painful my lessons have been, each person has played his or her part perfectly to propel me into more growth, understanding, and compassion in my life. All of them, as they have come and gone, have provided a tremendous gift: an opportunity for me to become clearer on who I am, what I want, who I want to become, what I will (and won't) put up with, and what I will accept as "the truth."

Time and the cycles of birth, death, and rebirth march on, no matter what we do, no matter how much we resist, no matter how much we beg for time to slow down. For example, I am now the matriarch of my entire family. It is hard to believe, really. I always had that "matriarch" place reserved for my grandmothers. Someday, I will be a grandmother myself, when my own children have children. These realizations can be overwhelming, and accepting the many cycles of our lives can be daunting.

But more and more, and for longer and longer periods of time, I notice that I am able to just *be*. I also notice that the more deeply connected to myself I feel, the more I have the serenity to not only embrace and celebrate change, but also to feel contentment and love. This quiet peace allows me to hear the inspiration in my heart, follow the intuition of my soul, and expand the dreams of my mind. It has been a rewarding journey, and I've discovered what brings me joy, what makes me laugh, and what gives me comfort.

*****

As this book comes to a close, I hope that together we can throw off the bowlines of the old ways of thinking and being in our lives, and in our collective sails, catch the trade winds that will move us gracefully into our new future of infinite choices and possibilities. I bless our spirits, which are always willing and able to explore new ways of thinking and being in the world. I bow in awe to our ability to dream big dreams and the courage we all possess to fulfill those dreams. And finally, I celebrate our capacity to discover how truly magnificent we are.

I'd be honored to hear your stories, thoughts, and opinions. Come join the discussion on my blog, at **www.WordsToThriveBy.com.**

Book Group Questions

These questions are designed to create dialogue, both within yourself and with your book group. Feel free to use these questions or to create your own! And if you would like to share your insights, please feel free to write to me at maryanne@ WordsToThriveBy.com or post them on my blog at www.WordsToThriveBy.com.

#1   Forgiveness

1) What does forgiveness mean to you?
2) Who or what in your life do you still need to forgive?
3) Try this: Look in the mirror and say, "I forgive you" to your reflection. How does that feel? What comes up for you?

#2   Gratitude

1) What are you most grateful for in your life right now?
2) "As you think, so shall you be." What is a new, more positive "mental word equivalent" for the you that you would like to become?
3) Try this: say the following to yourself along with a positive feeling, "Every day in every way my life is getting better and better." Did you believe it? Did you feel any resistance? If so, what was it?

#3   Determination

1) In what area of your life do you feel the most determined?
2) In what area of your life would you like to see more determination?
3) Do you agree with the statement, "If I believe in me, I can accomplish anything."? If so, what would you accomplish in your life right now. If not, why not?

#4   Respect

1) Reflect on this for a moment: Do you interrupt people around you on a regular basis? If so, who? Do you know why?
2) If not, is there someone in your life who constantly interrupts you? How does that make you feel?
3) Consider creating more awareness around becoming more respectful to both yourself and others. What could that look like?

#5   Comfort

1) Comfort can come to us in many different ways. What brings you comfort? Does comfort show up in your life in the form of a person, a place, an activity, a food, or in some other way? If so, what is your favorite comfort?

2) What could be a new comfort you would like to introduce in your life?

3) Try, including one comforting activity, conversation, destination, or recipe, in your life today. You deserve it!

#6 Courage

1) The original definition of courage is "to tell the story of who you are with your whole heart." Tell a story about one courageous moment in your life.

2) What's a moment in your life that you remember where you wished you had been able to find more courage within yourself, but didn't or were unable to. Close your eyes and imagine that moment again, and this time, bring your courage with you. Did anything change?

3) Where do you need more courage to show up in your life today?

#7 Joy

1) What has been a "sideways blessing" in your life?

2) How has that "sideways blessing" changed you?

3) There is only one of you on this entire planet. What is your purpose—recognized by yourself—as a mighty one? What is one small step you can take today towards fulfilling your unique and one-of-a-kind mighty purpose?

#8 Inspiration

1) What inspires you?

2) Try creating an "inspiration field trip" through your favorite bookstore or library. Did any book catch your attention? What happened?

3) What book or quote is the most inspiring for you?

#9 Transformation

1) Is there a part of you just waiting to "crack open" so something beautiful, unique and new can get out?

2) Do you dare to let that "something" out?

3) Have you considered asking for help? When you ask, help always comes.

#10 Peace

1) My biggest obstacle to my own attainment of peace is my relentless pursuit of perfection. What's yours?

2) The American rock guitarist, composer, and singer Jimi Hendrix said, "When the power of love overcomes the love of power, the world will know peace." Do you agree? If so, why? If not, why not?

3) What do you need to do right now to bring more peace into your life?

#11 Judgment

1) Have you perhaps judged yourself too harshly? If so, how?
2) If you could turn your judgment toward a more positive direction and take a courageous leap to try something you perhaps have always felt was out of your reach, what would you do?
3) If you don't have a dream to aspire to right now, why not create one?

#12 Power

1) Where do you feel most powerful in your life? Powerless?
2) Where does "healthy power" show up in your life?
3) Consider creating your own "Power Playlist" of songs, that make you feel powerful. Which songs would you choose?

#13 Wholeness

1) How can you become more at peace with change in your own life? Or in other words, how could you practice more non-resistance in your life?
2) If you were to ask for help with a current obstacle, what would be your question?
3) There are ancient labyrinths all over the world. In the United States, labyrinths are being built increasingly in churches, cathedrals, and wellness centers. Try to find a labyrinth near you.

   As you enter the labyrinth, think about what you would like to release in your life. When you get to the center of the labyrinth, give thanks for all that you have learned as a result of your obstacles or challenges. As you leave the center of the labyrinth and retrace your steps, imagine what you would like to bring more of into your life. Is it peace? Is it vibrant health? Is it love? Focus on what you would like to increase as you walk the labyrinth to the outside. After you leave the labyrinth, be mindful of what shows up or changes in your life.

#14 Dream

1) Many people have given up on their dreams at some point in their life. What is a dream in your life that you still long to have fulfilled?
2) What is one small step you can take today, towards fulfillment of that forgotten dream you put away, thinking it was impossible to achieve?
3) Again, never forget: if you can dream it, you can create it.

#15 Resilience

1) The Buddha said, "Change your thoughts and you change your world." What is one thing that you have believed about yourself that now, upon reflection, you realize is not actually true about you?
2) How would you live your life differently now if you believed this new and different truth about yourself?
3) What part of the resilient, strong, amazing you, would you like to reconnect with?

#16 Trust

1) Are you trustworthy?
2) Have you found yourself in a difficult situation because your have been too trusting? If so, what was it?
3) What would you do differently in the future?

#17 Love

1) Do you genuinely love yourself? If not, what change would you need to make in your life so it would be possible to truly love yourself?
2) Do you genuinely believe you are worthy of love and belonging?
3) Do you have the courage to allow yourself to be imperfect and to fully embrace your vulnerability so that you can allow yourself to be truly loved?

#18 Grace

1) Who in your personal or work life would you like to thank for the grace of their love and support?
2) Take a moment now to call, write, e-mail, or text them to say thank you.
3) If you were writing your own dictionary, how would you define grace?

#19 Humor

1) Can you relate to the Japanese proverb: "The tongue is but three inches long, but it can kill a man six feet tall."? Tell a story about when you took a "tongue lashing" and how you handled it.
2) What is your favorite joke? Take turns telling your favorite joke to each other.
3) What is a moment in your life when you laughed so hard, that you actually cried?

#20 Possibility

1) Where do you feel the most compelled to move forward into new possibilities in your life?

2) What is a time when the hairs on the back of your neck have stood up in warning? Did you listen? What happened when you either did or did not listen to your gut instinct about a person or a situation?

3) Holliwell said, "Obstacles seen from a higher view are stepping-stones instead." What is one obstacle you face right now that may look like a huge wall now, but if seen from a higher perspective, would only be another stepping-stone in your life? If you saw it not as a barrier but as a stepping-stone toward an infinite number of choices, what would be possible for you in your life?

#21 Hope

1) Where do you need more hope in your life?

2) It is said by the masters that "even a little poison can cause death, and even a tiny seed can become a huge tree." The Buddha said: "Do not overlook negative actions merely because they are small; however small a spark may be, it can burn down a haystack as big as a mountain." What is one action that you took in your life that caused such a spark that it "burned down a haystack as big as a mountain?" If you still have lingering guilt over this action of yours, is there anything you can do today to rectify or resolve it?

3) Similarly the Buddha said, " Do not overlook tiny good actions, thinking they are of no benefit; even tiny drops of water in the end will fill a huge vessel." What is an action you took in your life where you completely underestimated its benefit?

#22 Perspective

1) We don't ever have to allow ourselves to get attached to what an other person says to or about us. Just because they say anything doesn't make it true. Where in your life could you let go of your attachment to what someone else has said about you and simply say, "So you say."?

2) Woody Allen said, "Comedy is tragedy, plus time." Do you agree? Is there a story from your life where at the time it seemed tragic and now you can find some humor in it?

3) How has the saying "This too shall pass" been helpful to you?

#23 Truth

1) What is a truth about yourself that you are really proud of?
2) What is a current "truth about yourself" that you believe but which, in fact, may not be true?
3) Do you believe that you can change an old belief and see a new truth about yourself?

#24 Intuition

1) Ask your own intuition, "How can I become more empowered, stronger, and happier?"
2) Do you agree with Einstein when he said that he had "a feeling for the order lying behind the appearance" of things of this world?
3) William Wordsworth said "Faith is a passionate intuition." Where or how has your own "passionate intuition" revealed itself to you?

#25 Wish

1) Richard Bach said, "You are never given a wish without also being given the power to make it come true. You may have to work for it, however." What super power do you need right now in your life to make one of your own wishes come true?
2) If all that's missing to make your dream come true is "a little elbow grease" or a bit of "sweat equity," what would be your next best step?
3) Do you believe that wishes can come true?

#26 Connection

1) Do you believe your head or your heart is your "bigger brain"?
2) Tell a story about when you trusted your intuition and it lead you to an unexpected connection in your life.
3) What is one way you can think of to more deeply connect with yourself? With another person?

#27 Kindness

1) What is a special, perhaps even unexpected, moment of kindness that you remember in your life?
2) What is a meaningful gesture of kindness that you remember having given to someone else?
3) Who can you think of who would benefit from a gesture of kindness from you today?

#28 Acceptance

1) Where do you feel a sense of resistance in your life or work? What is one action you could take today that will move you towards more acceptance about that circumstance or person?

2) "The Work," created and taught by the teacher Byron Katie, is outlined on page 187. Pick a challenging situation in your life and ask yourself these four questions below:
   a. Is it true?
   b. Can you absolutely know that it's true?
   c. How do you react? What happens, when you believe that thought?
   d. Who would you be without the thought?

   Where did this journey lead for you? Do you feel any more acceptance of yourself or the challenging situation in your life?

3) In a split-second space between your thoughts, ask yourself, "Who is it that is observing all this drama in my life?"

#29 Rise

1) If you were a moth and you floated down on to a multicolored Persian rug right now, what color on the rug would you choose? How does that color make you feel?

2) If you could choose a different color, what color would you like to choose instead? Do you feel any different being surrounded by a different color?

3) Do you believe that there is never, ever, one moment wasted in your life that is not a part of your spiritual growth and development? If so, why? If not, why not?

#30 Integrity

1) What does living with integrity mean to you?

2) What do you think of the concept of *Ubuntu*?

3) How could you apply the principles of *Ubuntu* to your own life? To your community?

#31 Responsibility

1) We all make mistakes. How have you resolved one of your mistakes in a responsible way?

2) What's the most irresponsible thing you've ever done that you were unable or unwilling to or just didn't resolve? If you had it to do over again, what, if anything, would you change?

3) What has happened in your life when you have "paid attention to the clues."? What has happened in your life when you did not pay attention to "the clues."?

#32 Patience

1) Why do you think patience is so challenging?
2) What is a life long dream you have given up on? How might you revive or resurrect your interest in pursuing that dream?
3) When was the last time your received a hand written snail mail letter? Why not write a letter today?

#33 Honesty

1) Where in your life do you feel "stuck at the bottom of the barrel" and you can't get out?
2) What would it take for you to acknowledge, as former Alcatraz inmate Whitey Thompson did, that "I am the only person who got me in here and I am the only one who is going to get me out"?
3) Do you believe honesty is always the best policy?

#34 Change

1) How could you embrace change more willingly and with a greater sense of curiosity?
2) "The truth consists of creating an outlet so that the imprisoned splendor may escape," said Robert Browning. What is one "imprisoned splendor" of you just waiting to escape? How could you create an outlet so that the imprisoned splendor of you could become manifested?
3) If the only constant in this world is change, do you believe that how we embrace or resist these changes makes any the difference? How can you balance your life between one of resistance and acceptance?

#35 Rebirth

1) Do you agree with Lee Strasberg's statement "You don't have to be something. You just have to be."?
2) How could you embrace a more quite peace within yourself?
3) What is one way you could celebrate or discover how truly magnificent you are?

Further Reading

For a Reality Check:

The Power of Myth,
Joseph Campbell and Bill Moyers, Anchor (1991)

The Places that Scare You: A Guide to Fearlessness in Difficult Times,
Pema Chodron, Shambhala (2005)

A Thousand Names for Joy: Living in Harmony with the Way Things Are,
Byron Katie, Three Rivers Press (2008)

The Power of Now: A Guide to Spiritual Enlightenment,
Eckhart Tolle, New World Library (2004)

Why Faith Matters,
David J. Wolpe, HarperOne (2008)

For a New Perspective:

Food Matters: A Guide to Conscious Eating,
Mark Bittman, Simon & Schuster (2009)

Sacred Pampering Principles: An African-American Woman's Guide to Self-care, and Inner Renewal, Debrena Jackson Gandy, Harper Paperbacks (1998)

Purple Cow: Transform Your Business by Being Remarkable,
Seth Godin, Portfolio Hardcover (2009)

Writing a Woman's Life,
Carolyn G. Heilbrun, W. W. Norton & Company (2008)

Think and Grow Rich,
Napoleon Hill, Tribeca Books (2011)

The Biology of Belief: Unleashing the Power of Consciousness, Matter, & Miracles,
Bruce Lipton, Hay House (2011)

The Life Organizer: A Woman's Guide to a Mindful Year,
Jennifer Louden, New World Library (2007)

Healing and the Mind,
Bill Moyers, Main Street Books (1995)

Anam Cara,
John O'Donohue, Harper Collins (1998)

Molecules of Emotion: The Science Behind Mind-Body Medicine,
Candace B. Pert, Simon & Schuster (1999)

A Whole New Mind: Why Right-Brainers Will Rule the Future,
Daniel H. Pink, Riverhead Trade (2006)

The Thank You Economy,
Gary Vaynerchuk, Harper Business (2011)

For Inspiration:

The Soul of Rumi: A New Collection of Ecstatic Poems,
Coleman Barks, HarperOne (2002)

The Go-Giver: A Little Story About A Powerful Business Idea,
Bob Burg and John David Mann, Portfolio Hardcover (2007)

If Life is a Game These Are the Rules,
Dr. Cherie Carter-Scott, Crown Archetype (1998)

The Alchemist,
Paulo Coelho, HarperCollins (2006)

The Gift,
Hafiz, Penguin Compass (1999)

Bird by Bird: Some Instructions on Writing and Life,
Anne Lamott, Anchor (1995)

To Bless the Space Between Us: A Book of Blessings,
John O'Donohue, Doubleday (2008)

Dream Work,
Mary Oliver, Atlantic Monthly Press (1994)

The Little Prince,
Antoine de Saint-Exupéry, Reynal & Hitchcock (1943)

River Flow: New and Selected Poems 1984–2007,
David Whyte, Many Rivers Press (2007)

About the Author

Mary Anne Dorward, PCC,

is a speaker, author, coach, award-winning radio host and cancer survivor. She is committed to being a positive influence in the lives, organizations and companies she touches through her speaking and writing. She has coached leaders in the business and the not-for-profit communities to help them both gain visibility and raise millions of dollars.

Mary Anne's commitment to making the world a better place through her company, **My Real Voice**, extends beyond working with professionals to further their bottom line. She knows that the most important speech many of us give is a toast at a wedding, a eulogy, or for a dinner with friends. Mary Anne delights in working on projects of all scales, helping everyday speeches become extraordinary ones.

A graduate of the University of California, Berkeley, she is a veteran of the National Speakers Association, and Global Speakers Federation and has been a professional actress on stage, television, and radio since she was seventeen. Mary Anne thrives when helping people to unleash their real voice and learn how to become relaxed, commanding, and persuasive in front of any size audience.

Mary Anne lives in the Pacific Northwest and is an avid international traveler.

About the Speaker

As a professional speaking coach, **Mary Anne Dorward, PCC,** has helped hundreds of people give powerful and winning presentations. Her clients include politicians, CEO's, sports celebrities, and humanitarians.

Mary Anne has helped businesspeople across the country sharpen their ability to speak both strategically and authentically to their many different audiences —clients, investors, board members, employees, and the media.

A member of the National Speakers Association, Mary Anne has addressed hundreds of groups, delivering entertaining, educational and inspirational keynote speeches both nationally and internationally. A Professional Certified Coach, she also has the distinction of being a member of the Global Speakers Federation.

Her topics include:

Courage and the Can Opener

Mary Anne teaches new perspectives and strategies in her workshop on making choices, telling your genuine story with your real voice, and overcoming the fear of risk-taking not only in speech-giving, but also in daily life.

Words to Take with You

A deficit of self-confidence can be one of the biggest hurdles to overcome. Through this experience, you will learn to trust in yourself and embrace your own story as you start a new path towards self-empowerment.

The Voices in Your Head: From Chatter to Champion

There's a champ in all of us, in amongst The Chatter. Mary Anne will help you find yours.

The Joy Ambassador for Cancer

What happened the moment a minister challenged Mary Anne to find the joy in her cancer experience.

For more information, please visit www.myrealvoice.com, or e-mail Mary Anne at madorward@myrealvoice.com.

Made in the USA
Charleston, SC
07 February 2012